MARIAGE BLANC
and
THE HUNGER ARTIST
DEPARTS

Other plays by Tadeusz Różewicz in print:
The Card Index (also includes The Interrupted Act and Gone Out)
The Witnesses (also includes The Funny Old Man and The Old Woman
Broods)
Both volumes are translated by Adam Czerniawski and published by
Marion Boyars.

Poetry by Tadeusz Różewicz in print:
The Survivor and Other Poems, translated by M.J. Krynski and R.A.
Maguire, Princeton University Press, 1976.
Unease, translated by Victor Contoski, New Rivers Press, 1980
Conversation With the Prince and Other Poems, translated by Adam
Czerniawski, Anvil Press, 1982

MARIAGE BLANC
and
THE HUNGER ARTIST DEPARTS

TWO PLAYS BY
TADEUSZ RÓŻEWICZ

Translated by Adam Czerniawski

MARION BOYARS
LONDON · NEW YORK

Published in 1983 in Great Britain and the United States by
MARION BOYARS PUBLISHERS
18 Brewer Street, London W1R 4AS
and 457 Broome Street, New York, NY 10013

Distributed in the United States by The Scribner Book Companies, Inc.

Australian and New Zealand distribution by
Thomas C. Lothian Pty.
4-12 Tattersalls Lane, Melbourne, Victoria 3000.

British Library Cataloguing in Publication Data

Różewicz, Tadeusz
Mariage blanc; and, The hunger artist departs.
I. Title
891.8'527   PG7158.R63

ISBN 0-7145-2775-0 Cloth
ISBN 0-7145-2776-9 paper

Library of Congress Cataloging in Publication Data

Różewicz, Tadeusz.
  Mariage Blanc; and, The hunger artist departs.
    I. Różewicz, Tadeusz. Odejście Godomora..
English. 1982. II. Title.
PG7158.R63A24 1982   891.8'527   82-12859

Photoset in North Wales by Derek Doyle & Associates, Mold, Clwyd.
Printed in Great Britain

MARIAGE BLANC

First English Language production – April 1977,
Yale Repertory Theatre, USA.
Directed by Andrzej Wajda

BIANCA ... Carol Willard
PAULINE ... Blanche Baker
FATHER ... Eugene Troobmick
MOTHER ... Elzbieta Czezewska
COOK ... Alma Cuero
GRANDFATHER ... Alvin Epstein
BENJAMIN ... Stephen Rowe
MILKMAID AND WENCH ... Polina Klimovitskaya
AUNT ... Norma Brustein
MR. FELIX and THE HUNTSMAN ... William Roberts
Guest, servants, etc., David M. Grant, Douglas Simes, Timothy Hagan,
Roy B. Steinberg, Shaine Marinson, Patrizia Norcia, Julia Przsboś.

Sets and costumes ... Krystyna Zachwatowicz
Lighting ... William B. Warfel and Lewis Folden
Music consultant ... Paul Schierhorn
Movement consultant ... Carmen de Lavallade

THE CHARACTERS

BIANCA
PAULINE
FATHER
MOTHER
COOK
GRANDFATHER
BENJAMIN
MILKMAID
WENCH
AUNT
MR. FELIX
THE HUNTSMAN
guests, servants, etc.

TABLEAU 1
THE GIRLS' BEDROOM

A paraffin lamp with a pink shade stands on a little table between the beds. Midnight: the clock strikes the hour. After the ninth stroke, one of the girls stirs uneasily. After the last stroke there is silence. Then one of the girls slowly turns up the lamp. In the dim light one can see furniture, pictures on the walls and a cross. The girls' dresses are laid out on the chairs. A girl with loosely flowing hair is sitting on her bed in a white nightdress done up to the neck. The other one is asleep, her head under the eiderdown, but her leg is hanging out; a white fat leg uncovered up to the knee. It dangles from the bed, its toes touching the floor. The leg is 'alive' even though motionless.

BIANCA   (*turning her head towards the sleeping girl*) Pauline, (*pause*) Pauline, Pauline ... Can you hear me? You're pretending. Well, sleep on! Meanie! (*she reaches under the pillow and pulls out a book which she draws to the light. Lies down on her side and begins to read. Breaks off, listens for a moment to the sleeper's breathing*) Pauline, please say something. I'm so cold. I'd like to get warm next to you. I was dreaming that I was falling into a well. Cold water everywhere. I opened my mouth. Water was pouring into me through my every opening. I saw your face above the well and then I woke up, all covered in sweat like cold water.

BIANCA throws off her eiderdown and moves over to PAULINE's bed. Leans over PAULINE, touches the eiderdown, strokes PAULINE with her hand, walks around the bed and settles on a little rug.

BIANCA   (*Whispers*) Lina ... Please wake up ... I'll read to you.

Strokes PAULINE's foot with her hand and touches her calf with her lips. The leg stirs uneasily and withdraws under the eiderdown. BIANCA gets up and slowly pulls back the eiderdown. PAULINE murmurs in her sleep, turns over and wraps herself up in the eiderdown. Her head covered in a nightcap is now visible. BIANCA pulls the eiderdown off with a decisive movement. PAULINE is lying stretched out on her back in a long white nightdress rolled up to her knees. Her eyes are closed. A livid violet tongue slowly appears between her lips. When BIANCA leans over her, PAULINE sticks her tongue out fully.

BIANCA Pauline ... What's the matter? (*Clasps her hands*)

PAULINE (*in a rasping voice*) I poisoned myself for love of Benjamin. I am dying. Bibianna, say goodbye to Auntie, Grandpa and Cook ... You'll find the jar with the poison under the bed ... See you in Heaven, my poor Bibianna ... (*turns her head to one side*)

BIANCA looks under the bed

PAULINE (*laughs*) Mind you don't fall into the chamber pot!

BIANCA (*under the bed*) She's scoffed the lot ... selfish ... (*she crawls from under the bed holding a jar containing the remains of blackberry juice*) One of these days you'll die of stomach cramp from overeating. (*the jar in her hands, she sits astride PAULINE, looking at her big pasty face and drawing a beard and a moustache on it with the juice*) My kitty, my dolly. Lina, my little dumpling, open your tiny little eyes. Don't fall asleep.

(*PAULINE groans.*)

BIANCA (*places the jar on the bedside cabinet*) She's fallen asleep again! You revolting little dumpling! She's asleep again! Asleep?! You revolting dumpling! (*watches PAULINE who has now thrown back her arms and is pretending to snore*) What revolting hair, moustaches in her armpits, ugh. Wake up my prince, my sleeping knight, oh my princess ... wake up or I'll bite your nose off (*brings her mouth close to PAULINE'S face, gently tightening her teeth round PAULINE's nose*)

PAULINE (*sits up hiding her nose in her hands*) Give me back my nose, slug. Give me back my little nose, you horrid dead slug.

BIANCA (*carressing her belly*) Mmmmm ... Mmmmm ... Lina's little nose is nice, nice little nose ... sweet little potato.

PAULINE Your tummy is full of worms, you are stuffed with worms.

BIANCA (*covering her mouth with her hand*) I'll be sick if you don't shut up.

PAULINE When you're asleep, they crawl out of your nose and ears, long and white like spaghetti, they crawl out of your bottom.

BIANCA Revolting, revolting Lina. You have a moustache everywhere, under each armpit and down there under your tummy. Dumpling, my warm, darling little dumpling, I'm not angry with you.

(*PAULINE yawns*) Don't go off to sleep ... I'll read you something, shall I?

PAULINE   (*in an artificial voice as if she were imitating someone*) Your reading bores me to tears. Poetry I suppose ... willows, swallows, ophelias, camellias, roses and poses ...

BIANCA   Know something? I've got a cigar for you ...

PAULINE   On an empty stomach to make me vomit. And what is this book?

BIANCA   (*picks up a book from the floor*) May I lie next to you? It isn't poetry. It's a very queer book. We'll have to read it quickly so that Daddy won't notice it missing from the library. I began reading it on my own ... Pauline, are you asleep?

PAULINE   Alright then, start reading your fairy tales.

BIANCA   I'm so cold, I'm shivering like an aspen leaf.

PAULINE   Go on then. Read before I curse you, you caterpillar. People do invent strange words. You could make four mistakes in one word in a spelling test ...

BIANCA   You know what I saw in the summer-house yesterday? I almost lost my breath. I nearly died laughing ... (*BIANCA cuddles up to PAULINE*)

PAULINE   Go on, show it to me. (*takes the book from BIANCA, looks through it at first without interest, but suddenly begins to read attentively*) Well, really!

BIANCA   Didn't I tell you? You read it aloud first, then I will. You are very warm.

PAULINE   Alright, alright, you dear cold slug (*reads in a somewhat rasping voice, through her nose*) ... in women, in some four-handed small monkeys, in certain carnivors, in bears, hyenas, the white seal as well as the female daman, the vagina is partially or totally covered with a membrane which the penis penetrates during the first intercourse.

BIANCA   And what is this demon?

PAULINE   Not a demon, a daman ... but I don't know what that is either.

11

BIANCA   A queer name.

PAULINE   Know what? I suddenly feel hungry. I could eat a whole pig with trotters or even a daman.

BIANCA   I've got something hidden away for you, sheer delight.

PAULINE   What is it?

BIANCA   Something sweet, something white, something soft like you ... Guess!

PAULINE   Bibianna, stop torturing me ... I really am dying of hunger.

BIANCA   Don't die! (*jumps out of bed, runs up to the screen and a moment later emerges with a plateful of pudding, sits down on the bed with the plate on her knees*)

PAULINE   Oh my Bee ... My only one ... Bee ... Bee. What about a spoon? How am I to eat this? You never think in a practical way.

BIANCA   Why not use your hands ... or even your mouth, straight from the plate.

PAULINE   (*returns the book, takes the pudding dish and tries it with her tongue*) It's lemon-flavoured! Now I'll indulge, and you can read!

BIANCA   (*looking at her sister*) Don't eat so fast or you'll feel sick.

PAULINE, her mouth in the pudding, doesn't reply

BIANCA   (*reads*) Man is a placental mammal ... (*BIANCA occasionally strokes PAULINE'S head while she reads*) Consequently his genital organs and their employment is the same as in all other animals endowed with hair, nipples and a navel. Normally he is not totally covered in hair, but there is no single area on his body where hair could not grow ...

PAULINE   (*her mouth full of pudding*) On the palms as well?

BIANCA   (*bursts out laughing – reads on, laughing*) While on the head, under the arms and on the mons pubis both sexes have hair.

PAULINE   (*poking about in the dish with her finger, mumbling*) It's so boring with all these hairs. Hair everywhere ... in the soup, on the comb ...

BIANCA   But not on Grandpa's head ... (*laughs*)

PAULINE   It's as nauseating as liquorice ... Read some other bit (*licks her fingers*).

BIANCA   (*turns over a few pages and reads*) Before the Polynesians had turned to Christianity they had the habit of standing upright holding their scrotum in their two hands so that the member would dangle between their fingers. This was the pose of the savage dandy (*BIANCA breaks off, looks at PAULINE who is now licking the plate*) What is a savage dandy?

PAULINE   (*interrupting her licking*) Savage dandy is the name of the Polynesian member before conversion to Christianity.

BIANCA   What member?

PAULINE   The Polynesian member.

BIANCA   (*shrugging her shoulders, reads*) Some animals do not have a scrotum, as was already noted by Pliny.

PAULINE   Don't read that Pliny! (*PAULINE snatches the book away from BIANCA. Both girls slide under the eiderdown. Only the heads and shoulders are visible. PAULINE's nightcap is pulled to one side*) Oh, look, here is something interesting ... A calmel!

BIANCA   Not a calmel – a camel ... Anyway, we've had the camel.

PAULINE   Don't bother to listen then, I'll read it to myself ... This is interesting!

BIANCA   Selfish.

PAULINE   Slug.

BIANCA   Alright then, read.

PAULINE   The member of dromedaries and cats hooks back ... But that's impossible!

BIANCA   And how do you know?

PAULINE   Idiot ... holy innocent ... during erection the member rises and points forward ...

BIANCA   I ... I have no idea.

PAULINE   That what?

BIANCA   Surely the dromedary and the camel are the same, but how can you compare a cat to a camel?

13

PAULINE Oh, for Heaven's sake, surely a dromedary is a name for people in diplomatic service posted to the East and engaged in translating from foreign languages. I'm trying to remember the name of the friend the poet Slowacki* had. Szpic ... Szpic ... Surely, you know all this by heart. He held just such a post and shot himself in the head.

BIANCA Szpicnagel.*

PAULINE Szpicnagel ... You always interrupt in the most interesting place to show off your knowledge. (continues reading) ... ruminants and wild boars have slim members; solidungulates, namely elephants and seacows, have thick and round members (bursts out laughing) A cow with a member! That sounds like genuine science ... cows have udders.

BIANCA But this is a sea cow.

PAULINE What difference does that make? Cows must have udders.

BIANCA Evidently you don't milk a sea cow, so she doesn't need udders.

PAULINE Rudders, rudders! You don't milk Cook, but she has rudders all the same.

BIANCA Udders not rudders. It irritates me when you don't speak properly.

PAULINE Show-off, idiot. You show off just in order to stick a pin in me.

BIANCA Me? A pin?

PAULINE Anyway, what about that stupid Szpicnagel?

BIANCA Me trying to use Szpicnagel to hurt you? You really are despicable, Lina!

PAULINE Have a good look at yourself and you'll find a tiny little udder or two there.

BIANCA And do you have nipples?

PAULINE Yes, but you haven't, of course. Slugs don't have nipples.

BIANCA doesn't reply, and silently leaves PAULINE's bed. PAULINE throws the book after her. BIANCA silently turns off the light. The girls turn their backs to each other. The clock strikes the hour.

* Note: pronounced Swovatzki and Shpicnagel respectively

14

TABLEAU 2
GLASS AND CHINA

A drawing room in the Biedermeier style – or in no style at all. BIANCA's parents are having tea. He is hidden behind a newspaper, she is crunching macaroons and looking through a notebook. He is dressed in black, she in light colours and a bodice.

FATHER   God in Heaven, who could have expected it. It's incredible! ... Can you imagine it, Lizzie, Kazio Mizerski is dead.

MOTHER pays no attention, absorbed in inspecting the notebook. She talks to herself, shakes her head, as if surprised at what she has found there.

FATHER   Listen ... (*begins to read*) Kazimierz Mizerski, one of Poland's distinguished balneologists, and for many years director of the Truskawiec* Spa, died suddenly following a stroke at the age of fifty-three. Fifty-three years: that's three years younger than me ... Over the last fifteen years the development of the Spa was closely linked with his name.

MOTHER   (*to herself*) No ...

FATHER   Over a number of years the late Dr Mizerski was not only the director but also the lessee of the establishment and he retained the title of director even when the new owner of the establishment, Count Żultowski*. (*mumbles*) ... the late Dr Mizerski enjoyed popular respect and admiration. As regards the present-day development of Truskawiec, which was his particular concern, he has made a permanent contribution ...

MOTHER   (*agitated, gets up from the table and starts pacing the room, notebook in hand, pressing a hand to her brow*) No, no, no!

FATHER   (*reads*) As far as Polish balneology is concerned, the death of a man at the height of his strength and experience, a man both energetic and active ...

MOTHER   (*sitting at the table*) I ... this is beyond comprehension.

Note: pronounced Trooskavietz and Joowtorski respectively.

15

FATHER   The heart.

MOTHER *hands him the excercise book trailing pressed leaves and flowers.*

FATHER *takes the book, stares at MOTHER.*

MOTHER   Look!

FATHER   (*casually flicking through the book*) Is this Bianca's homework?

MOTHER   But she used to be such a healthy girl.

FATHER   What's the matter with her, then?

MOTHER   ... this looks like some poetry or other.

FATHER   Oh, well, let's have a look, calm down ... See here how this Kazik ... (*opens the book*)

MOTHER   She was a perfectly normal girl.

FATHER   (*reads in the same voice as if he was still reading the newspaper*) This is my first love ... even though so many, ah so many, kisses have burnt my lips. I love the most beautiful son of the earth, a splendid human beast with shining eyes and sleeping soul. I love disgustingly and wonderfully, I love and hate, I desire and despise (*murmurs some of the words*)

MOTHER   She was a healthy girl ... what's become of her.

FATHER   (*reads on in the same voice, but a little faster*) You have sullied me with your eyes and you must die. You have sullied me with blasphemies of words and there is no torture for you that is beyond my imagination (*shakes his head in disbelief*) oh, you who have been a rose in my hair, a holy chalice ...

MOTHER   This clearly has something to do with a man.

FATHER   ... A rose in my hair ... why can't I destroy you like a rose, like a chalice, like a heart ... roses? chalices? This and that, in a word, a school-girl's tittle-tattle, and you go into hysterics ...

MOTHER   Read ... please go on.

FATHER   On either side a dizzy abyss, behind me the desert I have traversed, baking in the sun yellow and naked. Death on a humped calmel gallops in pursuit. You have chosen your prey badly, calmel rider, my legs are swift, they have overcome many an obstacle; my head is strong like a pommegranate it will pierce a rock ... (*pauses in thought, glances at MOTHER*) Well, yes, perhaps indeed something's not quite so. Nolens volens, it doesn't make sense. Where has this humped "calmel" sprung from like a jack-in-a-box?

MOTHER   Oh God! Oh God! ...

FATHER   She must have seen a painting in Bremen and is fantasising now ... a humped camel!

MOTHER   Vincent ... I am afraid.

FATHER   (*now reads on with greater attentiveness, even puts a certain amount of "feeling" into some expressions, with an element of buffonery as if through that buffoonery he wished to calm his own anxiety*) Or I will jump behind you on the calmel, tear the bridle out of your hands and rush past with death at my side ... What in God's name is all this about the camel? ... The fact that she keeps writing "calmel", that's sheer perversity. She thinks that this makes her more of a literary person. She probably means not so much a humped camel as an ordinary one-hump or two-hump camel ... and she's got a hunchback instead! Of course she meant a dromadery and she got a hunchbacked calmel instead.

MOTHER   Vincent, I'm afraid what she means is a man.

FATHER   Don't be silly.

MOTHER   (*taking the excercise book from him*) Some dromedary! (*opens the book and reads in a passionate voice*) Oh the indescribable charm of a sun-burnt face. Oh sweet terror of purple lips and steely eyes ...

FATHER   Stuff and nonsense!

MOTHER   ...steely eyes. Whole days I keep my eyes closed in order to see them and get drunk on them. I run into the cave with a golden calf and pay divine hommage to the idol. (*MOTHER reads on with increasing excitement. She reads as if she herself has written and experienced this "stuff and nonsense". FATHER observes her with growing puzzlement. MOTHER speaks alternately with her eyes half-closed and staring at him "provocatively" ...*) I want to whip, whip, whip you, until I have whipped into you that unconditioned pain which arouses the spirit even in a beast. I want to torture you into a moan from the deepest abysses ... You know about it, you wonderful, stupid animal (*FATHER now looks uncertain*) ... You know it and you don't, because your brain rises above your trembling body like a molehill on a volcano ... You feel that terrifying flame in me ... (*COOK enters with a jug of cream on a tray. Oblivious of this, MOTHER continues to read with mounting excitement*) ... and that is why you run so fatefully like a maddened steed into a burning house. A viper of desires is clinging to my breasts and a lioness of ecstasy tears at my entrails ...

COOK (*aside*) Should be alright now ...

MOTHER I love the viper at my breasts and the lioness in my entrails.

COOK (*approaching the table*) I brought the cream you ordered, Madam ... (*puts the jug on the table*)

FATHER and MOTHER gradually regain their composure and a 'sense of reality'. FATHER picks up the paper, MOTHER pours out the cream. FATHER puts out his cigar, MOTHER opens a drawer, taking out some papers.

FATHER Quite a good photograph ... It's the image of Mizerski ... all the same, 53 years ... (*begins to read, hides behind his paper again*)

MOTHER (*after a pause*) Perhaps you ought to go and see Osinski? (*FATHER mumbles*) I think you ought to look up Osinski if you get the chance.

FATHER What was that? (*folds the paper*)

MOTHER We've got to make up the losses ... so many things get broken since last year. It really is quite frightening.

FATHER Last year we bought a whole crateful of glass.

MOTHER Don't you know in the kitchen it all slips through their hands. Even the dinner service has pieces missing.

FATHER Osinski is a terrible robber ... Fijalkowski * will sell you the same stuff only cheaper.

MOTHER But Vincent! Osinski has artistic products which could become a part of Bianca's trousseau. Fijalkowski has nothing fashionable and it would be nice to have something in the Secession style or the Highland manner. Osinski has good quality products and a refined taste. Fijalkowski's simply a glass and china warehouse.

* Note: pronounced Feeyawkovski

FATHER   My dearest, before Bee gets married we shall have more than one china set smashed. Meanwhile I have to buy a tine harrow and centrifuge.

MOTHER   But I can't use a centrifuge to serve at table, and besides you can count the service and the glass as part of Bianca's trousseau. I have chosen a set that is cheap and practical. Here! (*reads*) Beautiful dinner sets costing 60 and 50 roubles for 12 persons, best china, decorated with beautiful hand-painted flowers or with initials, comprising the following items: 36 flat plates, 12 soup plates, 12 pudding plates, 12 dessert bowls, 12 coffee cups with saucers, 12 tea cups with saucers, 1 tureen, 4 oval dishes, 2 round dishes, 2 fish dishes, 4 salad bowls, 2 gravy boats and 2 gravy spoons, a fruit bowl, 2 mustard sets, 2 salt cellars, 2 butter dishes, 1 coffee-pot or tea-pot. A total of 121 items.

FATHER   121 items!

MOTHER   The faience sets cost 34 roubles, and if you pay another 10 roubles, you get an extra 86 pieces of crystal glass ... But we couldn't use the faience as part of Bianca's trousseau.

FATHER   A stock of china. What a transport problem.

TABLEAU 3
THE CONFESSIONAL

Lighting of variable intensity; it grows and fades, at times goes out almost completely. An empty confessional stands against the background of a violet curtain in the middle of the stage (the drawing room). The stage in semi-darkness. BIANCA enters on tiptoe, in a white dress, a garland on her head, perhaps a bride's dress. Her face is barely distinguishable in the gloom, her hands move restlessly. She kneels at the confessional, her face covered with her hand.

BIANCA   I now see everything as unclean. In the garden, in the meadow, fat frogs mount one another, butterflies open their trembling white wings and raise their abdomens, they fly around coupled, and even flies ... I don't want to be a girl, I want to be a boy and have a member instead of an opening. I would like to be a soldier when I grow up, and a clergyman now, is that a sin ...?

They all laugh at me at home. So please tell me why I can't be a priest? Is it because I am a girl and only a man can be a parson? That means everything's been decided once and for all. Is it because I have a womb instead of a male member and a scrotum? Is that why any man may mount me? So anyone with a prick can be ... Only a bull, a boar, a stallion ... and us? We are the unclean vessels. They are clean, while those who bleed are unclean. How despicable, how silly this is. Naturally, they all laugh at me. Why can't parsons have bosoms? I don't know where I get these thoughts from. Do I have to chase them away through toil and prayer? I can't sleep. I hate father, I wish he were dead. He is no father, he is an animal. He chases all the women from the cowshed to the kitchen, from the kitchen to the drawing room. He assaults my mother. She is so tiny, like a bird. I heard her moan ... I am afraid he will break her. Men are like ...

A naked woman, her hair loose, runs along the back curtain. She is chased by BULL-FATHER foaming at the mouth. Otherwise he looks normal. They circle the confessional several times. BULL-FATHER kneels at the confessional.

BULL-FATHER   I am wretched, she is all china, dozy and cold, while I
burn. I despise myself and yet I desire them all. It's enough for
something to resemble the female shape. Age or colour makes no
difference to me.

*From time to time something creaks, grunts, squeals in the empty confessional.
These sounds are the voice of the non-existent confessor. GRANDFATHER
enters slowly, kneels with difficulty on the other side of the confessional, behind him
a barefooted MILKMAID, her skirt pulled up, a pail in her hand. Her blouse is
unbuttoned, showing a white breast. BULL-FATHER jumps up. The
MILKMAID runs off squeaking, followed by the bellowing BULL-FATHER.*

GRANDFATHER   I desire with all my heart, universally, in thought,
word and deed. Unclean, unclean – that is my drama. I thought
that old age ... old age would protect me, would build defensive
walls, ramparts and ditches around my body, that thinking about
life eternal beyond the grave would become my shield and
defence against temptations. But even greed has returned, and
gluttony and laziness. I am ashamed to say that it is like being in
high school again or a student, and I have become vain and
flirtatious. I dye my moustache and beard, and out of vanity I use
a wimper ...
   I thought I would immerse myself in a deep-blue old age, like
a cool crystal spring. While here am I, living in a warm thick
soup – to put it delicately. I find myself returning to bad old
habits I had 70 years ago ... (*GRANDFATHER demonstrates that
he again practices the sin of Onan*) This hand which ought to grip
the rudder on the soil, the hand of a plough, this hand
accustomed to the rapier and the pen. Everything tempts,
everything leads to temptation. Once again I find myself picking
raisins out of the cake, eating chocolates and fruit-gums. Instead
of taking my place in the pantheon I keep thinking about my
looks. I keep turning round, staring... those bottoms, those
darling nipples, those hams. I expected that I would be freed
from animal lusts and devote myself to meditation in a
hermitage. But it's no use. I shudder whenever I meditate on
eternal salvation and the grave. Death disgusts me. So will they
really push me into the earth and stamp on it?... shut me up in
my coffin? Wall me up in a tomb? They'll push me into the
earth and stamp on it. While here are all these darling bottoms so
wiggly and shapely. What an ass that naughty Pauline has now
... when you stroke it it's like a peach, when you pinch it, it's as

21

tough as a thong. Pat it and she turns and twists it ... turns it around me like a spinning top.

While GRANDFATHER is saying all this, PAULINE enters and begins to turn and twist. Behind her, the barefoot MILKMAID and COOK also twist and turn. GRANDFATHER follows them with his eyes, also twisting and turning his head. BULL-FATHER rushes in breathless. Kneels at the confessional.

BULL-FATHER I've come with an amendment (*suddenly jumps up and chases the MILKMAID who runs off, followed by BULL-FATHER*)

GRANDFATHER (*nodding his head*) It's the blood, the blood ... (*GRANDFATHER begins to mumble*)

A prolonged moan. It is MOTHER moaning for about 30 seconds before she reaches the confessional. The moan turns into quiet music — and at the same time MOTHER speaks in a melodious voice, charged with suffering.

MOTHER I can't bear this any longer. I'll take a drug or a potion. I'll stab myself. I never loved him, either when I was giving myself to him or when I was bearing his children. Inside I was always empty and cold. He was nothing to me, and now be has become hateful. I hate him, hate him, hate him.

Now when our child, our daughter, is about to become a wife, a woman, a mother, I find his advances repulsive and disgusting ... Faithfulness and obedience unto death. Ah, what do you know about the hell which a married woman finds in the bed of an unloved husband. I've been hating him since our wedding night, he arouses disgust in me ... just as then ... when I ran away to mother. They married me to him without asking my consent. They were afraid I would end up an old maid. There were 18 of us at home, 17 girls and one boy, the only boy Benjamin, who died of whooping cough in the army during the Leipzig campaign.

The placenta of the umbilical cord, leukorrhoea. Ah, ah, Father, if you had all that inside you like I have, you would sing a different tune. Certainly different! As for that tyrant of mine, he hasn't diminished his demands, quite the contrary ...

Silence for a few seconds. COOK enters. Sweating, she stands behind her mistress. Wipes her face with her apron. Listens attentively.

MOTHER Feet off the earth
along arcs of heaven
following stars of gold

with tears
of wonder joy and grief
I'll fly

COOK *kneels next to her mistress and speaks into her ear in a loud breathless whisper, wiping her face, her neck and her breasts with the apron*

COOK Will it please you madam that I rub the roast with garlic or tamarisk? Should I add marjoram to the joint and dill to the elder gentleman's camomile tea? Am I to wait until the roast gets brown on a slow flame and baste it when it's taken out, or as soon as it is in?

MOTHER (*pays no attention to COOK*) Please don't persuade me into submission ... a whole life of pregnancies ...

COOK The forester has just brought in a billy goat, so I don't know, am I to slaughter it and serve it with horseraddish and cold beetroot, or am I to pickle it in cuckoo-flower and vinegar? Will madam come into the kitchen for a minute, please? (*COOK kneels*) And he never lets me alone even when I am standing by the kitchen range. The other day I was adding cream to the tomato soup, and the master came upon me quiet-like from behind so I almost died of fright. I pulled myself together and I say, 'Aren't you ashamed sir, you have grown-up children, it is a grave sin from behind and I won't get absolution.' But the master takes no notice and gets on with it, and only when I began crying he moderated himself and began explaining to me. He pulls out a silver rouble and says: 'have a good look on this side, is it a rouble?' It is — so the master turns the rouble to the other side and again asks: 'and on this side, what is it?' Also a rouble, I say. 'There, you see, stupid! In front and behind it is the same rouble and the same arse, and so there is no sin.' He gave me the rouble and walked off. And there I was with that rouble standing and standing ...

MOTHER So it is through my abstinence that I am placing him in danger of sin? In other words, it is again my fault? But he isn't a youth. Cook, take roughly a kilo of the ham next to the kidneys, but make sure you wash it well, slice it into five equal portions, get the pestle damp in water and beat the meat on one side only. You know the way Master likes it. But remember to salt each cutlet on both sides at the last minute before frying. And don't forget to sieve the breadcrums thoroughly.

COOK   Madam knows I am familiar with the Master's tastes. Shall I also serve carrots and a salad?

MOTHER   Yes do, and place the cutlets in the long dish, arranging them one against the other, and pour sizzling butter over them.

TABLEAU 4
'OH COME ...'

The same drawing room. The furniture has been rearranged, so there is more open space. A summer evening, tree branches across the windows, dogs barking in the distance. Guests of different ages and dressed in various styles, but on the whole conforming to the fashions at the turn of the 19th century. Specific props: flower vases and pictures in the Secession style, but this should not be emphasised. BIANCA is sitting at the piano, playing some romantic piece. Next to the piano, a young man, dressed either in student uniform or in a party dress, turns over the music. The last few bars – applause. Now BIANCA'S MOTHER goes up to the student, takes his arm and says something to him. Hubbub of voices. He gesticulates in a protesting manner, but eventually bows his head. Rests his hand against the piano, looks up, looks down, waiting for the hubbub to subside. Recites.

BENJAMIN   Oh come!

come in autumn –
wearing a robe light, white, airy,
a spider's web;
cast on your auburn hair
pearls of dew
glistening with a rainbow
of cold hues ...
Oh come in autumn –
wrapped in the sad longing complaint
of cranes
flying aloft in the grey depth of heaven
breathing the scent
of flowers from which the frost
draws blood.
Oh come in autumn –
at twilight drowsy shimmering uncertain
and rest
your soft diaphanous scented hands
on my suffering
brow

Silence about 30 seconds. The 'poet' bows his head slightly and turns back to BIANCA. She too is clapping, but suddenly breaks off, there is surprise and fear in her face. Her mouth open, as if ready to scream. Between BENJAMIN's legs she observes a huge member like that of a horse. BIANCA covers her face with her hands and begins to squeak like a bird. MOTHER runs up to her and throws her arms around BIANCA. PAULINE also runs up and attempts to force BIANCA's hands from her face. The rest are frozen still. BIANCA laughs and cries, hiding her face in her MOTHER's bosom. MOTHER makes calming movements. With her arms still round BIANCA, she leads her out of the drawing room, followed by PAULINE, who is saying something, a smile on her face.

MOTHER   Please don't interrupt your enjoyment, she only feels a little faint.

After they are gone everybody remains still. FATHER is the first to move. He walks across to BENJAMIN and taps him on the shoulder.

FATHER   You have created such a mood. You have terrified us so with death. You see, it's not a poem fit for a social gathering. We are lucky not to have had all the other ladies fainting. Leave death to the Black Friars. And now I'll recite something:
Life is short. That is true.
Live, enjoy all you can –
Life means loving:.
Burn your books and grab a girl
Squeeze her tightly like a lemon

Laughter and applause

Stop the moralizing chatter!
Give up virtue when lust calls!

Two or three couples begin to dance. As the party begins to warm up, MOTHER, BIANCA, and PAULINE return to the drawing room. They sit down. BENJAMIN walks up to them, but BIANCA, as if terrified, runs across to the other side of the room next to GRANDFATHER. They are talking, laughing.

MOTHER   (*glances at BENJAMIN who smiles at her uncertainly*) Do enjoy yourselves. It was only a moment. It's her age. (*walks away*)

BENJAMIN   Miss Pauline, did you notice anything about me?

PAULINE surveys BENJAMIN from head to foot with an assumed gravity.

BENJAMIN   What happened? Why was Bianca terrified as if she had seen a ghost?

PAULINE   (*bursts out laughing*) She's got worms, poor girl. She's often sick, she vomits, but she is alright now.

BENJAMIN   But she ... but it's I who frightened her (*automatically checks all his buttons*) Perhaps you've noticed an untidiness in my dress, some departure from the norm?

PAULINE   You are funny... (*laughing, she runs over to GRAND-FATHER*)

BIANCA plays the piano with one finger.

GRANDFATHER   (*laughing, strokes BIANCA's head, PAULINE clasps her hands in supplication, appears to be asking for something*) Oh my little lambs, do you remember how you rode on my knees, one on this one, the other on that, eh? Want to go for a ride again?
  This is the way the lady rides, lady rides, lady rides,
        clip, clop, clip
  This is the way the gentleman rides, gentleman rides, gentleman rides,
        gallopy, gallopy, gallop
  This is the way the farmer rides, farmer rides, farmer rides,
        jogetty, jogetty, jog
  —and *down* in the ditch!

PAULINE   If I did sit on Grandpa's leg, it would break. (*laughs*)

BIANCA kneels at GRANDFATHER's feet and presses her head to his knee. Suddenly she sees his trousers rising as though something was trying to break through them. And slowly there sprouts a white member resembling a stinkhorn. BIANCA is the only one who sees this, she moves away in silence. GRANDFATHER watches her, puzzled. FATHER, smiling, walks up to him and offers him a cigar. PAULINE runs laughing to BIANCA who now stands at the window, her back to the guests. PAULINE embraces her, whispering something in her ear

FATHER   Aha! The other one runs away too. Grandpa's forgotten that the little lambs have grown into young ladies and are not interested to know how the farmer rides, unless they are Benjamin's or Felix's knees (*they laugh*).

The piano is heard again. The young men approach the girls. They bow and invite them to dance. PAULINE turns round and begins to dance. BIANCA continues to look through the window, motionless. Only after a moment does she turn and look terrified at the young man who stands to attention. Between his legs BIANCA sees a huge member like a stick. It seems that the young man is trying to pierce her. There is terror in BIANCA's face. Lights go out. A red bloody glow grows outside the window. A bell tolls. The whole drawing room is swamped in light, like red water. BULL-FATHER charges through the drawing room.

TABLEAU 5
BLOOD IN THE GIRLS' BEDROOM

The interior is grey. It is dawn and streaks of rising sun shine through the closed shutters. BIANCA stirs uneasily in the bed. PAULINE is asleep, uncovered. She has thrown her eiderdown on the floor. From time to time BIANCA moans in her sleep, moves and wakes. BIANCA pulls her hand from under the eiderdown, looks at it and hides it again under the eiderdown. A moment later she pulls out both her hands and sees blood on them. She sniffs them. She lies quite still. Slowly she removes the eiderdown, looks at herself, kneels on the bed, examines the bedclothes, touches her body, the blood-stained night-dress and the sheets. She sits up on the bed curled up, her legs gripped tightly with her arms, then she carefully lies down on her side and covers herself up with the eiderdown. She lies motionless. PAULINE tosses from side to side, embraces her pillow and snores occasionally. The clock strikes the hour: four times. BIANCA lifts up the eiderdown. Suddenly she jumps out of bed, squeals and then utters a continuous yelp, goes over to PAULINE's bed, pressing her hands against her belly.

PAULINE (*waking up*) Oh God, I am frozen! (*she bends over across the bed, pulls up the eiderdown, suddenly notices BIANCA and stares terrified at the blood stains*) What are you up to? (*BIANCA takes a step towards PAULINE. PAULINE moves back*) Why are you howling? What is it? You're all covered in blood.

BIANCA Something seems to have snapped inside me.

PAULINE (*getting up*) I'll fetch ...

BIANCA They haven't yet come back from the ball.

PAULINE (*jumping out of bed*) Lie down and stay there! (*rushes out*)

BIANCA stands motionless, her arms along her sides. Suddenly, with quick movements she pulls off the sheets and stuffs them into the stove. AUNT comes in, followed by PAULINE. AUNT embraces BIANCA and strokes her head. BIANCA is completely passive and dumb, PAULINE excited and involved.

AUNT Off to bed with you, Pauline, there is no point in running around in your night-dress, you'll catch cold. I'll see to things.

Come Bianca, be calm at all costs. Nothing's happened. You'll have to wash. (*they move behind the screen: sound of water being poured out, etc.*) Cotton wool! Where do you keep cotton wool?

PAULINE   I've made a beard and moustache out of it.

AUNT   Well, really ... (*in a little while AUNT and BIANCA come out from behind the screen, AUNT glances at the bed*) And where is the sheet?

BIANCA   I stuffed it into the stove.

AUNT   That was silly ...

AUNT changes BIANCA's bedding, while BIANCA stands motionless. AUNT tucks BIANCA in her bed, cuddles her in the eiderdown and kisses her.

BIANCA   I'm sorry ...

AUNT   You are silly ...

BIANCA   But ... I ...

AUNT   Well?

BIANCA   Please, I beg you Auntie, don't say anything to Daddy. You may tell Mummy, Cook and whoever you like, but not Daddy! Never! If you tell him, I'll kill you!

AUNT   Sleep, sleep. Goodnight, children.

AUNT goes out, the girls lie in silence for about 10 seconds.

BIANCA   Paulie ... (*silence*) Paulie ... are you asleep?

PAULINE   I'm asleep.

BIANCA (*after a pause*) Do I disgust you?

PAULINE doesn't reply.

BIANCA   Do I? Tell me ...

PAULINE still doesn't reply.

BIANCA   Aunt told me it will all be over in three days and I'll be just as I was before.

PAULINE   I have no idea.

BIANCA   Then we'll again be lying together, talking …

PAULINE doesn't reply.

BIANCA   Not today, later.

PAULINE again doesn't reply.

BIANCA   If you are good to me, I'll tell … (*after a pause, boastfully*) … I had a vision!

PAULINE   Liar.

BIANCA   I swear on Grandpapa's ashes, on Mummy's and Daddy's heads … St Nicholas came to me.

PAULINE   You're mad. St Nicholas isn't around in the summer.

BIANCA   I saw him, as I am seeing you. I could have touched him with my hand …

PAULINE   And when was that?

BIANCA   Perhaps three years ago now … when I was in bed with mumps.

PAULINE   So why didn't you tell me about it at the time?

BIANCA   I didn't dare (*bashful*) and also I lost faith. But as time passed I came to believe in my vision more and more deeply.

PAULINE   St Nicholas isn't around in the summer …

BIANCA   Where is he then?

PAULINE   Up your nose … An old cow like you still believing in fairy tales.

BIANCA   Of course I believe.

PAULINE   Go on believing them then.

BIANCA   You won't be granted absolution after what you've said about St Nicholas.

PAULINE   Listen, I feel itchy, as if an ant had got into my little groove.

BIANCA   (*begins to weep*) You pig, you pig … I'll tell everybody … I really did have this vision … Don't you believe me?

PAULINE   So maybe you're a saint?

BIANCA   So you do believe now that I did have a vision. I was lying alone because they had moved you to another room. I was lying alone, I remember everything well. Daddy and Mummy and Auntie, they all went away to see friends. So I begged Cook to come and see me, but she said she was busy getting the ducks. I lay for a very long time, thinking about various things, but mostly about a dress for holy communion, about our dresses and veils, the way we would march like two princesses all covered in lace and tuille. I was drowsy but I wasn't asleep. I swear on Grandpa's bones it wasn't a dream. I had my eyes closed. I heard someone turn the handle but no one was opening the door. I felt that somebody had entered through that closed door, as though a scented wind was blowing and a shape was floating towards me on the wave of this very beautiful perfume. I was pretending I was asleep, but through the slits in my eyelids I saw St Nicholas standing at the foot of the bed. He had a red cloak and a big white cap pulled so low that I couldn't see his face. He wasn't carrying a sackful of toys, he approached me, he bent over and gazed at me without a word. Then I closed my eyes tightly and pretended I was asleep. But he didn't move. I said Our Father once. Slowly I made a tiny slit and peared up. He bent over me as though he was listening to my breathing, and in a voice like beautiful music he asked, 'are you asleep my little child?' I didn't move but started to pray again in my mind. It was then that he stretched out his hands in red gloves and gently began to remove the eiderdown. I turned on my side. St Nicholas then dropped the eiderdown and stood upright. His head was touching the ceiling and the whole room was filled with his red cloak. I lay motionless. Then again I turned over on my back. He leant over me and gently began to lift up my night-dress. I was still praying and pretending to sleep.

PAULINE   Why were you pretending? You should have said something.

BIANCA   I didn't want to frighten him off.

PAULINE   Stupid, a vision like that wouldn't be afraid. You wanted him to look at you down there.

BIANCA   Pig ... I won't tell you any more.

PAULINE   Those who stop half-way end up in hell. Now I will tell you about my vision. Don't think you are the only one who has visions. Today I had a vision in the garden, in the raspberry bushes.

BIANCA   I lay there like a corpse, while he was pulling my nightdress higher and higher, almost right up to the neck. I had my eyes closed, but I felt ... Then I heard the gentle rustling of a robe, I peered up again and I saw him above me, leaning over, without a face, like a red bird. He wasn't saying anything, only gazing at me. I closed my eyes tight and I almost stopped breathing. I was listening to his strange heavy breathing. He breathed as heavily as a smith's bellows, like a tired horse, and I heard my heart beat. I couldn't move my hands or legs. I wanted to say something but couldn't. Then the clock struck twelve. I counted, and at the last stroke I opened my eyes and began to look at him. He was rising now, almost touching the ceiling and was gazing into my eyes through those slits in his cap. Suddenly he raised his red-gloved hand and made a sign. Then without opening the door, he walked out of the room. It was only after a while that I pulled down my nightdress and covered myself up with the eiderdown. I began to pray and then I fell asleep. (*silence*) Pauline?

PAULINE   Well?

BIANCA   Swear on your own head you will tell no one about this vision, and if you do, may you go blind, dumb and mangy ...

PAULINE   Amen. I swear. But I ... But I do know why I am always hungry when I wake up in the night ... And this Nicholas of yours, was he wearing trousers?

BIANCA   No.

TABLEAU 6
WEDDING AND MOURNING

An open trunk in the middle of the drawing room, bed linen and underclothes laid out over all the furniture. MOTHER and AUNT are sifting through the linen; they count it, sort it out, arrange it, unfold it and fold it. PAULINE is also present but she takes no part in the fuss and only cries out: 'how pretty, how divine'.

MOTHER   Three batiste day shirts: one white, pink (*hands it to AUNT*) and blue.

MOTHER hands each to AUNT in turns. AUNT fold the shirts, ties them up with a ribbon and puts them away on the table.

MOTHER   Three knitted day shirts (*counts them and hands them to AUNT*) and matching silk bloomers.

AUNT folds the shirts and bloomers and ties them up with a ribbon.

MOTHER   (*calls out in turn every piece of underclothing, inspects it, folds it and hands it to AUNT*). One modest petticoat in pink toile de soie with lace or tuille and matching bloomers in the same material.

PAULINE   Oh, how pretty!

MOTHER   One even more modest petticoat, black, to go with dark evening dresses.

PAULINE   Divine!

MOTHER   Four night shirts in batiste or toile de soie, some brassieres in matching colours ... (*they inspect the minute brassieres*)

PAULINE   (*trying one on*) It's so tiny it would fit a dove ...

AUNT   No need for you to worry about that Pauline ... when Bianca starts suckling ...

PAULINE   (*bursts out laughing*) Suckle, suckle, suckle ...

MOTHER wipes her face with a handkerchief. AUNT continues to sort out the

34

linen, interleaving it with lavender. Then sits down on the sofa. MOTHER is
arranging lace handkerchiefs, smoothing them with her hand.

MOTHER   May the Lord grant Bianca greater happiness in marriage
than her mother had.

AUNT   Pauline, please tell Cook to send us some nice tea with jam ...
But don't you eat up the jam on the way, you glutton ...

PAULINE laughs and runs out of the room.

AUNT   I must tell you in confidence that I am worried about the way
Bianca behaves. Her father brought her up like a boy, like a
soldier, she is not coquettish in the least. Obviously this mustn't
be overdone, but a little bit of vitality. A young girl shouldn't
shuffle like an old professor or be as stiff as a peg. There is no
softness in her movements. Even when she dances ... she won't
cuddle, she won't bend, she might have swallowed a stick. Poor
Mr Benjamin, he also becomes stiff when he is with her, as
though he were dipped in starch.

MOTHER   Perhaps she will change when she is married and warmed by
the rays of love. I think he is a sensible boy, I am confident about
the future.

AUNT   And did the rays of feeling soften you, warm you up, melt you?
The very same thing was being said when they were giving you
away to Vincent. He was so keen to get married he couldn't
stand still, and instead of a tinder-box he got a little angel, a
pretty but cold china angel.

MOTHER   Leave the past out of this, don't rake up the embers. I never
wanted to marry him. Vincent always seemed to me too fiery ...
I felt I couldn't satisfy him. I was convinced that only you could
make him happy ...

Silence for some 10 seconds. Then the women return to their jobs. This time
AUNT pulls out tablecloths and bed-linen from the trunk, and again both women
inspect, unfold and fold every item.

AUNT   Three coloured breakfast tablecloths, 2 white tablecloths with
napkins for 12 people, for larger gatherings, 2 smaller ones for 6
people, little coloured tablecloths for coffee and supper ...

MOTHER   For a family meal of 6, select the cream or the blue.

AUNT   Three changes of bed-linen, one elegant, 2 more modest, 12 Turkish towels, 12 kitchen cloths, 6 kitchen towels ...

MOTHER   I don't think we need rush with the dresses. The fashion changes so frequently. In any case, I think I ought to see our seamstress about that. For the time being she can manage with a black party dress, a dark skirt, some pretty blouses and two housecoats.

PAULINE enters carrying a tray with a tea-set, jam and pastries. She arranges it all on the little table, sits down in the corner of the sofa and eats the jam off the saucer, licking her lips occasionally. The women pour out the tea, drink, eat and talk.

AUNT   Pauline, do you have to smack your lips so much?

MOTHER   (*leafing through a magazine*) Perhaps I shouldn't be saying this, but after all, there are matters one can't ignore, so one ought to talk about them openly and straightforwardly, as one does about other matters that touch on life ... (*browsing through the magazine*). I think I've found something more suitable ... Look, Angela.

AUNT moves over closer, they now both look at the magazine, while PAULINE continues to sample the jam.

AUNT   Daddykins is growing weaker all the time and the worst may happen at any moment, but he hasn't got the least idea.

MOTHER   Maybe it is just as well for him. But we must remain brave and clear-sighted on his account. After all, buying the material and even the preparation means nothing. I knew people who after the last unction lived on for another ten years. Bah! Not just lived, but indulged themselves. I think this mourning dress in matt silk with draperies on the collarbone and the lace ruffle would suit me. An 80 centimetre width isn't a lot either, making it some 3 metres and a little over.

AUNT   For us at our age these draperies look too bright ... too provocative.

MOTHER   So, maybe this one in georgette, trimmed with ruches at the neck and sleeves. Draperies on the bodice ... with a 90 centimetre width we would only need 3 metres 39 centimetres. Perhaps you would choose that other one? The girls could have two similar dresses. Those!

AUNT   Perhaps we ought to ask … Pauline, stop licking out that saucer and come and have a look … here … A dress in crepe satin with trimmings in white silk with black dots …

PAULINE   And when is Grandpapa's funeral?

MOTHER   How can you?!

PAULINE   Me?

MOTHER   This is sheer cynicism and lack of manners.

PAULINE   I'm sorry.

MOTHER   There are unfortunately many people who regard the wearing of mourning as a convention, but it is difficult to imagine one's closest relatives walking behind the coffin of their father or brother in colourful and gaudy attire.

AUNT   When you grow up, Pauline, you will understand that for us women …

PAULINE   But Grandpapa is as healthy as a mushroom. He was capering around the garden like a grasshopper.

MOTHER   What do you mean by capering?

PAULINE   Well, just simply that he was playing at chasing Cook. And he even jumped on top of her.

AUNT   Don't babble and don't interrupt. Well then, we women do not need to lose our charm even during mourning. What's more, you ought to know that the black of mourning often brings out a woman's beauty. A woman who looked banal and insignificant in a colourful dress, suddenly appears ravishingly pretty in mourning.

MOTHER   There are many instances of this.

AUNT   A suitable hat with a long veil is most important during mourning.

MOTHER   A veil is a blessing for many women.

AUNT   For amongst them there are those who desire to hide their grief as deeply as possible.

MOTHER   And tears especially.

AUNT   From the aggressive and penetrating looks of improper persons.

MOTHER   Beside the hat you must also think about the rest of your dress.

AUNT   Most suitable for a dress is wool and crepe silk, and in the summer georgette, muslin and chiffon.

MOTHER   Matt shoes, preferably suede.

PAULINE   And sometimes I imagine that Auntie or Uncle has died or that everybody has died ...

MOTHER   (*slaps her on the face*) Apologize at once!

PAULINE   I apologize.

MILKMAID runs across the stage in wooden clogs, her blouse unbuttoned over her breasts, followed by BULL-FATHER, followed by Cook in bloomers and bra, followed by GRANDFATHER leaping. The women don't interrupt their conversation. They have not noticed the procession. Only PAULINE's face registers surprize ... she may have noticed ... but it isn't certain.

MOTHER   After the first six months of mourning white is allowed.

AUNT   So one can decorate black dresses with white collars, frills, cuffs and stripes, and on hot days one can wear all white. During this period one also stops wearing hats with veils, replacing them with black hats.

MOTHER   Simple ones, with white feathers, flowers or similar decorations.

AUNT   One starts wearing pearls and diamonds.

MOTHER   Excluding coloured jewellery.

AUNT   Mourning following the death of parents or a spouse is worn for a year and six weeks.

MOTHER   Mourning for grandparents lasts six months.

GRANDFATHER enters despondently. He gazes around wildly. The women, engrossed in the magazine, don't notice him. GRANDFATHER kneels with difficulty as though at a confessional which isn't there. Strikes his breast, etc.

GRANDFATHER   (*as if continuing his earlier confession*) ... the silent kingdom of death is powerful and mysterious. It's idle to resist it. From among the numerous dogmas, this one most terrifyingly and mercilessly proclaims the very end of earthly life. Although on the other hand, as if in recompense for the above, it throws to the world the triumphal truth regarding the new and more perfect life beyond the grave ... (*MOTHER puts a finger to her lips ... The three women leave*) I imagined that white hair, the dignity of age, would be my defence, in that as an old but faithful fighter I would not only serve grandchildren and greatgrandchildren, but that at the end I would undividedly give myself up to serve the nation and the people, that my helping hand would extend to the peasant and the tradesman, the craftsman and the groom ...

TABLEAU 7
IN A BLACK WOOD

Past and Present

The scenery is almost operatic. Grey and black treetops and treetrunks, their branches invisible. Here and there green ferns sprout from the black undergrowth. A beam of light pierces the space between the treetrunks or falls from above. The light illuminates only the central part of the wood, and it is dark on the peripheries. Multi-coloured mushrooms lie hidden in the darkness. It is a fairy tale forest. Silence. Two girls in white dresses walk and run around the trees. In this light we cannot discern their faces, the emphasis is on the whiteness and movement which may have the character of a game. They bend over as though they were picking mushrooms or bilberries. The girls look for each other, call to each other, stop to listen and disappear from view. For a moment the forest is empty and after a pause only one girl enters − BIANCA.

BIANCA   Pauline! Lina! Yoo, hoo (*10 seconds' pause*) Yooo Hooo! Answer me!

Music. A man wrapped in a black cloak emerges from the darkness. He runs across the stage and stops, his back to the audience. The girl − BIANCA— her face towards the audience − stops frozen still. The man stretches his arms widely, opening the cloak. BIANCA stands still. She covers her face with her hands. Suddenly she tears herself away and runs among the trees and bushes, ripping her muslin veil. The man moves his arms up and down several times, as if he wanted to fly away. Light fades, the man disappears in the darkness. Now light grows again. Pauline enters the forest holding a basket.

PAULINE   Yooo Hooo, I'm here, yooo hooo (*listens*) Answer me. Bibi! Yoo Hoo!

BIANCA enters. Her dress is smeared, torn, her hair dishevelled. She runs up to PAULINE, covers her with her arms. They are entwined together in an embrace.

PAULINE   (*after a pause*) What's the matter? You're so changed, your heart's pounding. What's the matter?

BIANCA clutching her more tightly, remains silent.

PAULINE   We'll go home, I think you're ill, you're trembling all over, are you cold?

BIANCA   Yes.

PAULINE   You're all in a sweat, and damp. What's frightened you?

BIANCA   I don't know.

PAULINE   Did you see a wild animal?

BIANCA   Yes ... yes ...

PAULINE   (*touching her face and forehead*) It must have been a wild boar.

BIANCA   I don't know.

PAULINE   The branches must have frightened you.

BIANCA   I ... Lina ... I saw ... (*presses her lips to PAULINE's ear*)

PAULINE   No! What do you mean?

Light fades. Music grows in intensity for a moment. Then silence. Light grows, illuminating a depleted forest, as if someone had chopped down some of the trees: a clearing, with white cloths spread on the grass. COOK and AUNT are busy getting mugs, saucers, napkins and food out of baskets. GRANDFATHER is talking to MOTHER. The rest of the company: the girls, MR FELIX, BENJAMIN, a black-dressed HUNTSMAN whose shape resembles the stranger's from the previous scene, are wandering amongst the trees. They are looking for mushrooms. Amongst the trees one can see red fly-agarics and various other toadstools and mushrooms, all of them of gigantic fairy-tale size. BULL-FATHER emerges from the forest. He prances around COOK in a suspect way, who chases him away with a cloth. MR FELIX, the land administrator, approaches BULL-FATHER. They converse.

MR FELIX   I'm not sure, your honour, I'm not sure. I think we ought not to buy yet.

BULL-FATHER   The back is quite sinewy.

MR FELIX   But the thighs are not so sinewy.

BULL-FATHER   So long as the loins ...

MR FELIX   The black one is well developed.

BULL-FATHER   It seems that the thighs and shanks are a little weak.

MR FELIX   I did feel her all over – I can guarantee ... the shoulder-blades and the back are well sinewed, the rump fully rounded. What else can one expect?

BULL-FATHER Slaughter and don't linger.

MR FELIX That is what I thought.

BULL-FATHER *pats MR FELIX on the shoulder, they move on.*

MOTHER Leave the past out of it, Angela (*polishing the glasses*). No use raking up the embers now, they have cooled. I had no wish to marry Vincent. If you remember, I knelt before you and begged you to save me from that yoke, that bliss ... but was that possible in those days? You would have been happy together, I'm sure. You always impressed him that, winter or summer, you never wore bloomers.

AUNT Not even now. It's both healthy and comfortable.

MOTHER Quite so.

AUNT You stand with your legs apart and it feels good.

MOTHER That's precisely what attracted him.

AUNT I was never an angel pretending to be gathering violets when I was going about a natural function. My dear Lizzie, I haven't changed in the slightest, naturalia non sunt for me turpia. But I do have Bianca's happiness at heart. It's probably the only thing in the world ... after all, I suckled her ... and I didn't want Vincent. By then I didn't want anyone. You know well what happened to my marriage. Michael perished in action, literally in the act of consummating our union. But such were the times; he had hardly mounted when the bugle called to horse, and before there was time to say 'charge' the bugle called them to dismount. So I was left holding a candle with a garland askew on my brow.

AUNT *is arranging meat on the plates, in the background BIANCA and BENJAMIN pass, holding hands, followed by PAULINE with a basket.*

MOTHER Let the shades be! We now live in peaceful times, let Bianca taste what we were not allowed to taste.

AUNT You have had children by Vincent.

MOTHER But I never felt a woman with him ...

The women's dialogue turns into gaggling cries accompanied by gestures. COOK

42

grunts from time to time. This applies to other dialogues: the conversation between GRANDFATHER and FATHER turns into grunts, groans, belches and laughter. Where the dialogues appear drawn-out they should be spoken quickly and turned into inarticulate sounds. The choice of appropriate episodes will depend on how the action is developing. BIANCA and BENJAMIN cross the stage talking.

BIANCA   I sometimes stare long into the fire and see his soul, tiny like a spark. But a spark which suddenly grows and rebels, which explodes and covers the trees, the forest, the house and the whole world. The fire turns into a tiger and devours the whole world. I'm turned into a handful of ashes, fire is a god, water is a goddess. Water covers everything. Sometimes I feel that it fills the whole room, that, cold and slippery like a snake, it tears into me through all the openings.

BENJAMIN   My dear Bianca, both water and fire, subdued by man, are his useful and obedient servants.

PAULINE runs up to them with a dance-like step. She is clutching a white stem of a toadstool. The stem has the thickness of an elbow and tapers into a conic head of a bluish-green colour.

PAULINE   Look what I've found! See how big it is! (*BIANCA and BENJAMIN stop*) ... isn't it beautiful? ... huge ... do you know anything about mushrooms, Mr Ben? I've never seen one like this ...

BIANCA   (*softly*) A strange shape ...

BENJAMIN   Do please throw it away, Miss Lina.

PAULINE   No! No! You're jealous, Mr Ben. But I'll show it to everyone. After all, we are supposed to be electing the mushroom queen.

BENJAMIN   That is a poisonous toadstool, please drop it and trample on it, then clean your hands thoroughly. You shouldn't be holding it in your little hands.

BIANCA   What a revolting smell it has! You're right ... Mr Ben, do you know what it's called?

BENJAMIN   Well, many years ago I studied at Heidelberg. I even began writing a doctorate thesis on the subject of mushrooms. My supervisor, dear old Pilz, was walking on air. He would pat me on the back and repeat ad nauseam: 'ins Schwarze getroffen,

43

ins Schwarze getroffen', but I got bored with the dissertation and came home. As a matter of fact, the mushroom you've found is ithyphallus impudicus from the family of phallaceae.

PAULINE   Do you have to complicate everything so? Bianca, look how strange it is. (*She hands the stinkhorn to BIANCA who throws it on the ground in disgust and tramples on it*) You wretch, you pig! She's furious because I found it and not she! (*BIANCA runs away*)

BENJAMIN   Putting it bluntly, Miss Lina, that was the shameless stinkhorn. It's an inedible toadstool on account of its very unpleasant odour, and has no culinary value.

PAULINE   It reminds me of something.

BENJAMIN   Let's join the rest of the company in case they think ill of us.

PAULINE   (*poking a finger in her mouth*) It reminds me of something. I know! I know!

BENJAMIN   Please calm down, Miss Lina.

PAULINE   It's you, it's you, you are ithyphallus impudicus. I can't stand you! I'll tell everyone what they taught you at Heidelberg!

BENJAMIN   But Lina ...

PAULINE   As far as you are concerned, I am Pauline. Please don't use diminutives. I hate it when a strange man does that.

BENJAMIN   (*gripping BIANCA'S arm*) Forgive me ... (*kisses her hand*)

PAULINE   Have you asked for Bianca's hand?

BENJAMIN   Yes.

PAULINE   Poor Mr Benjamin.

BENJAMIN   Poor?

VOICES   (*hands clapping, voices calling*) Yoo Hooo! Teatime! Please come! Where are they?

PAULINE   Poor, poor Ben.

BENJAMIN   Quite the contrary, I feel very rich, a maharajah.

PAULINE   Poor.

BENJAMIN (*irritated*) But why? What do you mean?

PAULINE (*runs away skipping, singing*) Poor Ben, big Ben.
  (*BENJAMIN follows her towards the company*)

AUNTIE now only cackles, and her cackling expresses everything: puzzlement, joy, doubt. She turns – cackling – to BENJAMIN – and everyone responds to the cackling as though they understood what it meant.

PAULINE I'm the mushroom-gathering queen!

GRANDFATHER And where is the mushroom?

PAULINE I found ... a splendid ... huge ... Bianca can testify ...

BIANCA is silent.

PAULINE It's because she's jealous ... it was huge ... colossal like ...

GRANDFATHER Well, well!

PAULINE (*bends her arm at the elbow*) Like this! (*demonstrates*) Mr
  Benjamin can witness!

AUNTIE cackles questioningly to BENJAMIN and her lips, now overgrown with thick, dark fluff, begin to look like a hen's arse: pink and improper.

BENJAMIN (*evasively*) Well, an agaric ...

PAULINE Angelic?

BENJAMIN Yes ... well ... of course ... an angelic toadstool ...

PAULINE Dogstool? ... Oh no, no, you won't deprive me of my
  queen's title ... And it was you, Mr Ben, who called it phallus
  impudicus.

AUNTIE cackles in horror, almost choking.

MOTHER (*quickly draws the conversation away from an embarrassing topic*)
  Mr Benjamin, breast or leg?

BENJAMIN, in confusion, rubs his hands.

MOTHER Please make up your mind. I recommend the breast.

BENJAMIN Indeed ... well, yes ... a leg, madam, although a breast ...

GRANDFATHER (*throwing a leg bone behind him*) As for me, my dear
  sir, it's the rump. The rump, I prefer the rump above all else.

(GRANDFATHER is given a rump, licks it, smacks his lips and drools)

COOK bursts out laughing and covers her face with her hand.

BENJAMIN *(sitting down on a treetrunk, eats the leg and recites at the same time)*
Let us go hence: the night is now at hand;
The day is overworn, the birds all flown;
And we have reaped the crops the gods have sown;
Despair and death; deep darkness o'er the land
Broods like an owl ...

BIANCA shudders and shakes herself. COOK again laughs, her hand at her mouth.

BENJAMIN I am haunted by spectres and mysterious crimes. The winged Ahuras of paradise are singing ...

COOK begins to wiggle and giggle strangely.

MOTHER *(sternly)* Are you ill, Cook?

COOK *(her face behind her apron)* Ah well, Madam, Ah well ... when Mr Benjamin says something ... you could wet yourself laughing ... "Ahuras" ...

GRANDFATHER *(sucking the rump)* Well, sir, it's soft, fatty, gooey and delicate. All the best flavours are in the rump, not the head ...

They now all sit down to eat. BULL-FATHER with MR FELIX, the land administrator. BULL-FATHER has a bull's head but is otherwise dressed normally, in a hunting outfit. Occasionally he bellows, laughs. Hunting horns are heard. The sun slowly sets. Red light drowns the black wood.

TABLEAU 8
SWEETS

The girls' bedroom, the night lamp is burning. PAULINE is holding a plate of pastries on her chest. Throughout the scene she keeps eating, drinking and licking.

PAULINE   Now tell me everything ... how did Benjie propose to you? Did he kneel in front of you?

BIANCA is silent, her face hidden in the shadows.

PAULINE   They'll take you away from me, my ladybird. Do tell me, I'm burning with curiosity ...

BIANCA   You know, Paulie, he was terribly embarrassed, he couldn't splutter a word. I said nothing. He took my hand in his. There was the silence of a temple. We gazed into each other's eyes.

PAULINE   They always start by holding hands. And then something else ... I must tell you that Grandpa is as delicate as your Benjie. He too mutters about a temple.

BIANCA   Grandpa?

PAULINE   (*sits up on her bed*) Well, imagine, last week, after the rehearsal, when everybody had gone, Grandpa began flirtatiously at first, but then quite seriously: 'Would you barter with me, Paulie? I'll give you this box of handmade chocolates and you'll give me ... ' (*PAULINE burst out laughing*) ... 'and you'll give me ...'

BIANCA   Well, well what?

PAULINE   (*repeats*) 'I'll give you this box of handmade chocolates ... cherry liqueuers and rum truffles, marzipans and candied fruit ... and you will give me ... ' well! guess! If you guess I'll give you half the box and you'll be able to come to my bed ...

BIANCA   You seem to have imagined something filthy, or he wanted you to give him a kiss.

PAULINE   No.

BIANCA   Did he want to put his hand under your skirts?

PAULINE   No.

BIANCA   Wanted to touch you there?

PAULINE   No, no, no.

BIANCA   Then I don't know.

PAULINE   He asked me for a stocking.

BIANCA   Just one?

PAULINE   Yes, one stocking.

BIANCA   And what is he going to do with it?

PAULINE   I don't know, maybe he's gone soft. He ran off to his room and brought a box as huge as a sieve, untied the ribbon and opened it, so that I could see inside. I remembered I had darned stockings ready to be thrown away, those black silk ones, I could give them to him, both of them. I could explain I gave them away in the village. In any case, they've been lying in the locker for months, and there he is already on his knees begging for the stocking ... asking me to put it on, take it off and other tricks like that. I felt like laughing, but he had such a look, I got frightened. I felt awkward because they were unwashed and stank ... And there he was kneeling and saying 'straight off your tiny foot, my little child.'

BIANCA   He must be going out of his mind ...

PAULINE   Wait. (*from under her pillow she pulls out a huge chocolate box tied with a pink ribbon, unties the ribbon, opens the box*) Look.

BIANCA   (*gets up, sits on the edge of PAULINE's bed*) Magnificent.

PAULINE   They are full of liqueuers and rum. I've already had half of them, last night when you were asleep. I was nearly sick ... my head was spinning with all that alcohol ... have one.

BIANCA   No, thanks. I'll have worms incubating in my guts ...

PAULINE   These are liqueur ones, the worms will die. If you try one you'll ask for more.

BIANCA   (*taking a chocolate*) But you haven't finished about that' stocking.

PAULINE   And you haven't told me how Benjamin proposed to you.

BIANCA   But I've just told you, he was holding my hand and couldn't force out a word ...

PAULINE   Silly-billy. Grandpa stroked my leg, and when I asked him whether I ought to wash the stocking because it stinks ... he burst out with a cry: 'No, no, let it smell of your tiny little foot'.

BIANCA   (*looks incredulously at PAULINE who is eating up the chocolates, suddenly both girls begin to laugh*) And then?

PAULINE   He kissed the stocking.

BIANCA   That I won't believe.

PAULINE   I swear on the ashes of my parents. Then he folded the stocking and put it away together with his wallet in his breast-pocket.

BIANCA   This I just won't believe under any circumstances. And where is the other stocking? Have you thrown it away?

PAULINE   Don't be silly! I put it away in reserve. When he loses the one off the left foot, he'll want to exchange something for that other one. He even remarked ... but give me your word of honour you won't tell anyone because he said if I did tell anyone something dreadful will happen to me.

BIANCA   Word of honour.

PAULINE   He said solemnly that one day he'll ask for my bloomers ...

BIANCA   Bloomers?

PAULINE   As I love you, bloomers. (*The girls eat the chocolates in silence as if wondering what GRANDFATHER might want with PAULINE's bloomers*) If you want, I could give you the other stocking as my wedding gift.

BIANCA   You can stuff it up your nose. You know, I think that my head is beginning to spin with all that liqueur.

PAULINE closes the box and hides it under her pillow.

BIANCA   Paulie … may I put my head on your tummy? … I feel so sick …

PAULINE   But don't press or I'll burst.

BIANCA   (*touches Pauline's belly with her fingers*) Your belly's stretched tight as a drum.

PAULINE   Have you ever slept on a drum?

BIANCA   No, that's just a saying.

PAULINE   I'm blown up like a cow with clover … what did I eat?

BIANCA   You eat without stopping all day … your lips make smacking noises even when you're asleep.

PAULINE   I am not a nymph or a watersprite feeding on poetry and weeds.

BIANCA   Shall I read you what I've written about our engagement?

PAULINE   A slug like you can live on flowers. You can eat two camelias – ophelias and three tuber roses for lunch and a lily or willow leaves for pudding, as they do in those poems … (*belches*)

BIANCA   So I'll read it to you.

PAULINE   Go on … it will send me to sleep.

BIANCA   In that case I won't … (*at the same time pulls out a notebook, and after a pause begins to read*) I have come to dwell with thee at the bottom of a lake in a golden temple like a bell, which thou wilt swing into action with arms powerful like branches of a tree. And the dead heart will stir the heart of the bell, to hold thy heart in my hand like a terrified bird. The heart beats and breaks with happiness. I wish to carry thee as a dromedary carries a leopard when the leopard buries itself in the cloth-of-gold of the dromedary's humped body. With my claws I will swing thy silent bell … Do you like this?

PAULINE   (*mumbles*) Hmmmmm …

BIANCA   (*carries on reading*) Oh bellringer of my temple! Swing with thy bronze heart the silent bell of my body, climb with me to the top of Mont Blanc and wrap me up with the flame of thy desire.

Oh thou beautiful, white, reeking like the shameless stinkhorn plucked in a black wood on St John's eve. Wake me, wake me, wake me!

PAULINE   (*yawns*) Beautiful.

BIANCA   I feel so cold ... may I press my cheek against your tummy ... (*PAULINE takes off her night-shirt, BIANCA presses her face against PAULINE's tummy*) It's so cosy ...

PAULINE remains silent.

BIANCA   What a darling little drum you have, silky ... may I kiss you? Today your navel's popped up, it looks like a cherry. Don't you think the navel is a strange part of the anatomy? What is it for, anyway?

PAULINE   I don't know. In any case surely the navel is not a part of the body like a hand or a foot?

BIANCA   What then?

PAULINE   Nothing. Why should you find the navel strange? You're fantasizing again. In fact, you're a big liar and you don't see anything. Try fooling Mr Ben with your vision, not me.

BIANCA   (*cuddles PAULINE*) If only you knew how your tummy rumbles, bubbles and spills about. It's so funny.

PAULINE   Don't press or I'll blow off in your face.

BIANCA   Pig.

PAULINE   (*sits up and pushes BIANCA away*) You silly thing. Do you want the gases to tear me apart? When I'm on my own, I break wind as well as a stable-lad ...

BIANCA   How dare you speak to me like that? You're cruel.

PAULINE   Blah, blah, blah ... I suppose in your case you have skylarks removing it from your insides. They've turned us into china dollies. We don't even have guts in our bellies. Surely you have to evacuate noxious gases, otherwise you'll burst or get cramp in your belly. Once, my skylark, I overheard the men sleeping in the stable after the hunt. They farted like horses. Each time they farted, they laughed as though it was a big joke.

BIANCA   Stop it.

PAULINE   And your Benjie was there too. I tell you, Bian, I think men don't differ much from animals. They've turned us into butterflies and little angels, but it's curious how such a bull or stallion wants to impregnate a butterfly. We have nothing, we are ashamed even of our own bodies, while they run around with their stinkhorns protruding almost outside ...

BIANCA   Lina, I beg you ...

PAULINE   I promised myself, I swore on the ashes of our mutual nurse, that one of these days in the drawing room at a reception or during a dance or when there is music and recitation I'll fart like a peasant, and then I can go to the monastery or die on the spot. But let the fools see that I am human like everybody else and not a watersprite of jelly and rainbow. There are gases in the temple of my body.

BIANCA   (*weeps*) What are you saying? Such ... you ... I

PAULINE   Bibianna, what is it? You're crying. (*embraces her*) Bianca, my dearest, I didn't want to offend you but sometimes I get so angry. I said that not because I was angry with you but with them. They want to separate us forever, they don't care about our feelings. They are giving you away in marriage, they want to push me out of the house with my studies as an excuse. They order us about as if we were calves or ducklings, but we too are humans. They pretend it's out of love they give away our bodies to the first man who asks for our hand, and it isn't a hand either, Bianca, they talk of hands but have the arse in mind. Our virginity is supposedly revered; they persuade us that the virtue of virginity is the greatest treasure, and then they give away those treasures to the first one that comes. All those saintly virginal martyrs ... take even those we are staging in our theatre, St Christine or St Agatha; they are fried in oil, they allow their breasts, legs, tongues and heads to be cut off but they won't give up their virginity or their faith. And whenever we hear the word virgin we blush because everyone from Grandpa to Bull-Father makes silly faces when they hear it. Don't cry, Bee, give me a kiss instead, you poor cold slug. That Benjie of yours will get a shock when he sees ... touches ...

BIANCA   (*puts her hand on PAULINE's mouth*) During our engagement I
            told him that I'll give him my hand if he is going to respect my
            views and my body ...

PAULINE   And what did he say?

BIANCA   Nothing. He grew pensive, there was a glazed look in his
            eyes. He stroked my head. He then swore he wouldn't hurt my
            feelings, when I told him that our marriage ... that we ... in a
            word that I wished for a 'mariage blanc'.

PAULINE   You and your silly 'mariage blanc'. Ask Cook what that
            'blanc' is really like ...

BIANCA   He swore that until I desire it, he won't touch me. Know
            what? I'll ask him that you too should come on our honeymoon.
            That'll be a treat. I beg you ...

PAULINE   You're rambling. Better show me your tongue.

BIANCA pokes out her tongue.

PAULINE   And now say 'aaa'!

BIANCA   Aaa!

PAULINE   Again!

BIANCA   Aaa! Aaa! ... why do you want me to show my tongue?

PAULINE   I don't know ... you are such a fool: aaa, bee ...

TABLEAU 9
DESCRIPTION

The drawing room. BIANCA stands in front of the mirror, covering and uncovering her face. She touches the reflection of her face in the mirror with her. fingers.

BIANCA   Le nez gros, (*touches the nose with her fingers, pulls it up, squashes it, squeezes it, and so on*) la bouche ordinaire, (*tightens her lips, smiles, shows her teeth, stretches her mouth with her fingers, sticks her tongue out*) la taille de trois ou quatre pieds de haut, (*turns her back to the mirror*) en un mot, c'est un petit monstre qu'est ta soeur Bianca.

BIANCA sits down on the sofa with her eyes closed, then slowly unbuttons her blouse and examines her breasts attentively; covering them with her hands, stroking them with her fingers, holding them in her palms as though she was weighing them … wrapped in thought she slowly buttons up her blouse. Now perhaps she falls asleep. In these scenes it is not clear whether they are happening in a dream or only in BIANCA's mind: a part of her reminiscences and desires. BULL-FATHER enters. He wears a jacket and a bull's head. He looks around, stops at the window, his hands in his pockets, motionless, silent. The light fades. BIANCA speaks in a monotonous voice as if it didn't belong to her.

BIANCA   I am getting married or rather you are giving me away. Perhaps at a moment like this you might be prepared to listen to your daughter who is to be transformed tomorrow into a woman. We have been moving away from each other over the years. You, shut up in yourself, I, given over to my dreams. I know that when little Erasmus died you wanted a son. You stopped talking to us, you kept silent for a number of years. You were disappointed and had little enthusiasm for my first cries in this world. When the midwife wanted to show you a child of the female sex, you turned away in disgust … you shut yourself up in your study, then silence again. In order not to irritate you, mother brought me up and dressed me like a boy until I was ten.

When as an adolescent girl I wished to confide in you, to embrace you, you would turn away and talk half-jokingly of 'a school-girl smelling of buttered rolls.'

MOTHER enters. She begins her monologue behind the door before she enters so that her words mingle with BIANCA's in one stream.

MOTHER   You all think that I am … that I don't exist … that there are no longings in me and the spring has dried up. But I desire. Despite six cradles, five coffins and nine pregnancies about which you know nothing. I never felt myself a woman carrying you. I lay under him like a tortured animal, like a stone. I thought that he must eventually understand, get discouraged by the lack of response … that he'll leave me in peace at last, but no … he is not satisfied with wenches, chambermaids, cooks, neighbours, big city cabarets, foreign … even now, he forces himself drunk into my bedroom and takes no notice whether I am ill, indisposed. His vitality is terrifying. They say he is a picture of health … indeed he overflows with health, and not just with health either, quite repulsively …

BIANCA   (*moves towards BULL-FATHER with an outstretched hand*) Father …

BULL-FATHER   Don't touch me …

The light changes. The interior is bathed in red light like blood. BULL-FATHER slowly turns away from the window, lowers his head. COOK, MILKMAID, AUNT and a few other undressed women run through the room, dancing. MOTHER clasps her hands in prayer. BULL-FATHER turns towards MOTHER. MOTHER retreats, hides behind the furniture, BULL-FATHER chases her.

Now BIANCA, or some other actress, runs onto the stage dressed as a torreador holding a rapier and, instead of the red rag, a white marriage veil. The corrida begins. BULL-FATHER tramples the veil. BIANCA sticks the rapier in his side. BULL-FATHER spouts blood, kneels on one knee, and eventually falls to the ground.

BULL-FATHER   (*in a rasping voice*) What have I done to you, my little daughter?

BULL-FATHER dies. The light slowly fades, then it is normal daylight. BIANCA is sleeping on the sofa. AUNT enters and wraps a shawl round BIANCA. AUNT then sits down at the table and plays patience. BENJAMIN enters, AUNT signals him to be quiet, then shows him the chair next to her. She is grimacing with her lips in a strange way, red lips surrounded with black hair which look very ambiguous. BENJAMIN stares at these improper lips as if spellbound.

AUNT *(looking at the cards)* You haven't loved yet, Benjamin.

BENJAMIN remains silent.

AUNT One can feel that. One can see it, but don't ... I am now beyond such matters ...

BENJAMIN But ... you still have ...

AUNT I have nothing, my kitten. Don't bother with compliments ... leave that for others. What I have I have ... as you can see ...

BENJAMIN I do ...

AUNT In a word, you haven't loved before.

BENJAMIN Well, in fact it's difficult ... well ... because of a peculiar set of circumstances I have remained pure, Madam. Then the very power of the matured instinct protected me from temptations *(moves closer to AUNT)*. For whenever with an unconscious sensual intention I tried to approach a woman I would be thrown into such confusion that everything was lost in it ...

AUNT *(takes BENJAMIN's hand in hers)* I have no idea what you did in those Heidelbergs of yours and have no wish to know ...

GRANDFATHER enters and seeing the couple wants to withdraw. Seems strangely embarrassed. He carries a large parcel wrapped in paper, or a big box tied with a pink ribbon.

GRANDFATHER Oh pardon, I seem to be interrupting ...

AUNT Good morning, I haven't seen you today, Father ... *(GRANDFATHER stands hesitating)* On the contrary, you may be able to help us, Father ... *(AUNT tries to take the parcel from GRANDFATHER but he hold it firmly against his chest)*

GRANDFATHER No ... no ... of course, I shall be pleased to help ... but I am only here for a minute.

AUNT That must be a wedding present for the young couple.

GRANDFATHER   God's blessing on the young bare ... Ooops! What was it I was going to say? I don't know whether Mr Felix has repaired the chaff-cutter yet. No, it's not a present.

AUNT   Then, what is it you are clutching Father? We were talking about Bianca.

GRANDFATHER   Yes, indeed, she does stoop a little. But don't let that worry you, Benjamin. Well, I won't interrupt any more ... (*Again GRANDFATHER attempts to sneak away, but this time AUNT presses him to sit down on the chair. GRANDFATHER absent-minded and embarrassed keeps looking towards the door as if he were expecting someone. Holds the parcel on his knee*) Mr Benjamin, when I was Bianca's age, I too used to stoop like some dromedary ... but young girls always try to hide their darling breasts ... in the first phase of their development ... especially when the breasts grow faster than those of their peers ... kyphosis pudendum ... sometimes the habit of a bad pose will become established. So do pay attention to that, Benjamin ... sometime later normally a little hair begins to appear on the mons veneris ... and later still in the armpits ... well, yes, I really must go ... farewell ... it's completely natural ... I wish you luck ...

AUNT   What on earth are you rambling on about, Father, Bianca's past all that.

GRANDFATHER   Is that so? Really? ... so what was I saying ? ... (*pats BENJAMIN on the shoulder*) Head upright! (Bianca stoops and draws in her shoulders) she is simply bashful. She's lost her poise ... but that will pass ... at her age a girl doesn't know what to do with her hands and feet ... which, by the way, can be livid, red or even marbled ... but in a twinkling the princess ... all this is due to a malfunctioning of the vessels beneath the epidermis ... in a twinkling a girl's profile changes, her pelvis expands ... (*GRANDFATHER talks to himself dreamily*) Female shapes ... curvatures ... for the moment she's still smelling of buttered rolls ... (*gets up, clutching his parcel and goes out*)

AUNT   (*waving her hand*) Allegorically ... my boy ... the flower of the soul should be so treated as not to wound it or snap it ... there are no rules ... (*barefooted WENCH runs across the stage followed by BULL-FATHER*) So you haven't loved before?

BENJAMIN   Yes, the circumstances have been such that I haven't loved, although … I have put it all into poetry …

AUNT   It's time you took it out … that capital of feelings…

BENJAMIN   (*springs up and recites*)
> I cry your mercy, pity – love – aye, love!
> Merciful love that tantalizes not,
> One-thoughted, never-wandering, guileless love,
> Unmask'd, and being seen – without a blot!
> O! let me have thee whole – all – all – be mine!
> That shape, that fairness, that sweet minor zest
> Of love, your kiss – those hands, those eyes divine,
> That warm, white, lucent, million-pleasured breast –
> Yourself – your soul – in pity give me all,
> Withhold no atom's atom, or I die,
> Or living on perhaps, your wretched thrall,
> Forget, in the mist of idle misery,
> Life's purposes – the palate of my mind
> Losing its gust, and my ambition blind!

The half-undressed WENCH again runs across the drawing room, pursued by BULL-FATHER. AUNT and BENJAMIN ignore them

AUNT   (*after a pause*) Mariage blanc … mariage … blanc …

TABLEAU 10
THE BRIDE'S TROUSSEAU

The girls' bedroom.

BIANCA   This is our last night together ...

PAULINE sits in a night-dress on her bed, pulling on long black boots. Gets up, pulls up her night-shirt and walks over to the mirror.

BIANCA   (*following PAULINE with her eyes*) What's all this show? Are you wearing boots in bed?

PAULINE   It's a present from Grandpa ... riding boots ... he also gave me this whip to match. And in exchange for all this, all he asked was that I should put these boots on in his presence or play horses with him. I thought I'd die laughing ... he wanted to get engaged to me ...

BIANCA   Paulie, how can you do such things.

PAULINE   But I am not doing anything. It's him ... keeps begging me, kissing my hands ... he's so shy ... as though he'd never loved. It's enough for me to straddle my legs on the chair and he begins to blush and stammer, and when he peers down there, it's as though he's having a vision. What does he see there? ... that's not my business but I won't allow him to touch me 'there'. Sometimes I pretend I don't feel when he puts his hand there and suddenly I smack his paw! Once he started crying ...

BIANCA   How can you, that's a mortal sin.

PAULINE   I don't do anything, I don't even move.

BIANCA   Animals ...

PAULINE   And when you get married, what then? What will you do? Tend flowers?

BIANCA   Ben swore he wouldn't touch me.

PAULINE   I'm sure he won't touch. But, my butterfly, how do you expect the children to arrive? For the children to arrive the male has to penetrate you with that male organ of his.

BIANCA   (*covering her ears*) No, no, no.

PAULINE   Yes, yes, yes.

BIANCA   Is it a large thing?

PAULINE   Like that of a horse ...

BIANCA   It won't fit into me then.

PAULINE   You little slug, you are hardly big enough for a needle, but in a real woman ... Cook has a hole like a fur hat ...

BIANCA   I can't be married. He'll thrust through me and kill me.

PAULINE   Women do often die as a result. But you can cut it off on your wedding night.

BIANCA   (*runs over to PAULINE and embraces her*) I am afraid ...

The girls lie in bed. They lie in each other's arms. PAULINE is eating or sucking something. PAULINE falls asleep. The hour strikes. BIANCA leaves the bed. She opens the wardrobe with linen. She spreads out the linen and the underclothes on the sofa and the table; her whole trousseau, including tablecloths, napkins and so on. She handles each item in turn ... calls out its name and tears it up. She throws the shredded linen onto a pile. She does all this in a passion but doesn't lose control. Some items offer resistance and then BIANCA used her teeth. She tears up: 3 white batiste day shirts: white, pink and blue; 3 knitted day shirts and matching silk bloomers, one modest petticoat in pink toile de soie, with lace, and a more dressy black petticoat, 4 nightshirts, several brassieres. Exhausted, she sits down on the edge of the sofa. After a pause she proceeds to destroy the bed linen. She struggles with the sheets and towels. From under her pillow she pulls out big tailor's scissors. She systematically cuts up each item. While all this is going on, PAULINE wakes and silently watches BIANCA: she seems paralysed. She sits up in her bed motionless. BIANCA does not look at her. She performs her task swiftly, as if in a trance, meticulously, attentively. She is now cutting up the tablecloths for 12 people. Terrified, PAULINE lies down and ducks under the eiderdown. BIANCA has finished the work. She arranges the cut-up linen and ties it up with ribbons. She locks up the wardrobe.

BIANCA   (*loudly*) The bride's trousseau. (*gets into bed and covers herself up*)

TABLEAU 11
THE REHEARSAL

The drawing room. The furniture is rearranged, amongst the furniture various bits of theatrical props: silver columns, a throne, some rugs, armour, instruments of torture, etc. PAULINE is sitting on the sofa. BENJAMIN is standing by the piano: with one finger he keeps strumming the same phrase of a song. On the table a silver helmet of a Roman soldier, coloured papers strewn on the floor.

BENJAMIN   Isn't anyone else going to come?

PAULINE   Bianca is indisposed. She's lying down. Grandpa has excused himself. In any case we don't need him in the first tableau ... we'll manage somehow ... Bianca's tongue is all furry, and white like cream cheese.

PAULINE goes up to the door, turns the key and hides it.

BENJAMIN   Shouldn't we leave it open?

PAULINE   Never. We might have someone undesirable and indiscreet peering in and spoiling the surprise. Surely, our performance is supposed to be a complete surprise for everyone ... for every one. Have you got your part?

BENJAMIN   I know it by heart.

PAULINE   (*looking around*) Where are the instruments of torture? (*she pulls out a wooden saw and a sword, both covered in silver paper*) For the time being I'll take Bianca's part and play St Febronia.

BENJAMIN   I know Lisymachus's role. But I don't know whether, without Selenus ...

PAULINE   Let's forget Selenus. I've already told you, Grandpa isn't available today. I'm ready. For the time being use the sofa instead of the throne. Let's begin!

BENJAMIN   Whereupon Selenus perceiving the steadfastness of St Febronia ordered that her robes be removed from her ...

PAULINE undoes the poppers and takes off her blouse, and a moment later her skirt as well. BENJAMIN is silent.

PAULINE   (*kneels in front of him, hands in supplication*) Oh, preserve me in purity and virginity. Do with my body whatever thou wishest but let my virgin soul survive.

BENJAMIN   Shall I speak for Selenus?

PAULINE   Speak for whoever you like, Mr Ben.(*removes her slip*)

BENJAMIN   Let the robes be removed! What are you doing, Miss Pauline ...

PAULINE   You can see, can't you? Please undo the clasps. (*turns her back to him*) What are you up to? Haven't you ever undone a clasp? (*takes off her bodice and covers her breasts with her hands*). Why are you gaping so, Mr Benjamin? Please speak your part and don't stare at me.

BENJAMIN   (*hesitating*) Let her be stretched out (*grunts and swallows hard*) and let her be hung on four poles. Let the fire be made ready beneath her.

PAULINE stretches herself on the chair, her bottom arched towards BENJAMIN. BENJAMIN stares silently, devouring her with his eyes.

PAULINE   Have you gone dumb, Mr Benjamin? Oh God, do I have to draw every word out of you?

BENJAMIN silent, approaches PAULINE from the back.

PAULINE   What are you doing there? Ah, so long as my purity is safe and my virginity is safe I care naught for fires and tortures. Heaven awaits me.

BENJAMIN   (*moves back*) Here again we have the part of Grandpa, that is, of Selenus: 'strikes her with birches'.

PAULINE   They are behind the cupboard, silvered!

BENJAMIN pretends to strike her back gently.

PAULINE   Harder, on the bum.

BENJAMIN strikes her bum.

PAULINE   (*sings*) Strike with your birch
           A bride of the church

My body you burn
But my soul will earn
Prizes in Heaven
Selenus in his pride
Will not force the bride
To worship a heathen
(*pause*) Now it's your turn, Mr Ben.

BENJAMIN   (*sits down on the sofa, wipes his brow with a handkerchief and breathes heavily*) Let her belly and her breasts be scorched!

PAULINE gets up from the chair and stands before BENJAMIN.

BENJAMIN   (*his head bowed*) Cut off her maiden breasts.

PAULINE takes his hand and touches her breasts with it.

PAULINE   Though half alive
I pray and I strive
To retain inviolate
My pure virgin state

BENJAMIN   Cut out her tongue and stop her chatter.

PAULINE angrily thrusts out her tongue at BENJAMIN.

BENJAMIN   But ... well ... I (*stammers*)

PAULINE   Have you lost your tongue?

BENJAMIN   Hang that female carcass on a tree!

PAULINE   (*lifts her arms, displaying her hairy armpits*)

The temple of my flesh
You may take if you wish
But my soul shall be
Unsullied and free

This doesn't seem to make sense, don't you think, Mr Benjamin? I don't think Bianca's idea of a temple has quite come off. Even my tongue's all exhausted ...

BENJAMIN   No ... no ... Lina ... what we are doing here under the pretext of a rehearsal isn't worthy of us ... and in relation to my fiancée ... I think we've gone too far ...

PAULINE   (*sits down on BENJAMIN's knees and shuts his mouth with her hand*) Poor Lisymachus. Poor, a hundredfold poor Mr Benjamin. He doesn't know what's in store for him. I've known Bianca since she was a child ... neither her soul nor her b ... I mean her body ... we have no secrets from one another ... Bianca often wakes up in the night with terrible screams. She says that in the night water pours into her through all her openings. She keeps running to my bed because her hands and feet are cold. She is all cold and sweaty like a dead frog.

BENJAMIN Lina ... Miss Lina, how can you? She loves you so much ...

PAULINE (*crying out*) She?! She's got worms! (*jumps off BENJAMIN's knee, suddenly runs to the door and puts a finger to her lips*) Shshsh! Shshsh! Quiet ... I think Grandpa's been peeping at us. (*does up her bodice, puts on her slip and blouse, etc − at the same time BENJAMIN is speaking*)

BENJAMIN Please be quiet. We've opened our souls to one another. Bianca has opened wide for me the temple of her soul.

PAULINE Idiot ... and did Bianca tell you that she has ... that she hasn't ...?

BENJAMIN What? You are ... you are corrupt to the very marrow.

PAULINE Quite the contrary, every bit of me is pretty. Ask Grandpa.

BENJAMIN Come to the point ... so what? What's Grandfather to do with it?

PAULINE If you wish, Mr Benjamin. Well, she has ... or rather she hasn't, but I heard Aunt telling Mother that so far you haven't loved.

BENJAMIN Miss Pauline! Or rather Messalina ... I ? I simply don't believe my own ears ... such words ... from such pretty lips.

PAULINE Yes, indeed, from these. Bianca has only one opening. Ten years ago when we used to play with little Erasmus...

BENJAMIN With whom?

PAULINE With little Erasmus, Bianca's dead little bother. As children, we used to play doctors. Even in those days he could stuff a whole finger into me, whereas in Bianca's case this little finger would hardly go in. (*shows BENJAMIN her little finger*) It almost broke. And BIANCA's belly is full of white worms. Her bum is as cold as an icicle. Poor Lisymachus, he'll get his limbs frost-bitten in his bedchamber.

PAULINE goes to the door and unlocks it. She is now fully dressed. BENJAMIN is standing at the window, speechless. PAULINE goes out.

BENJAMIN (*at the window*) Aspasia … Messalina … Vagina … it's beyond all understanding…

GRANDFATHER peeps into the drawing room cautiously. He is holding a big parcel or a box.

GRANDFATHER Good morning you haven't seen the little Pauline here?

BENJAMIN is silent.

GRANDFATHER She said she would be waiting for me here … with the rehearsal.

BENJAMIN (*without turning*) The rehearsal is over now.

GRANDFATHER Oh, she's deceived me so, the flighty wretch, but she's got a heart of gold … developed above her age … she hasn't said where she was going? Into the garden? … perhaps she's seeing Bianca. What's the matter?

BENJAMIN is silent

GRANDFATHER God's will and testament … and where might she be … she's like a drill, Mr Benjamin, turning and twisting … (*goes out*)

BENJAMIN (*his back still turned, presses his face against the window pane and after a pause speaks to himself*)

> I cried for madder music and for stronger wine,
> But when the feast is finished and the lamps expire,
> Then fall thy shadow, Cynara! the night is thine;
> And I am desolate and sick of an old passion,
> Yea hungry for the lips of my desire…

MUSIC

TABLEAU 12
THE HAPPY PAIR!

The light fluctuates. This is a 'realistic' scene but not real. Music. Table covered with a white cloth and decorated with 'garlands'. Table set for 12. Crystals. Wedding guests. All the people who appeared in previous tableaux are sitting round the table. The actors utter voices and sounds, they say whatever comes to their heads. They speak with the voices of domestic and wild animals, smack their lips, belch, murmur, bellow and raise toasts. Some guests are wearing masks. Men have noses whose shape resembles male members of varying length and colour. These nose-phalluses dangle over the plates. GRANDFATHER dips his long wrinkled nose in a sauce. Only BULL-FATHER's nose is raised high, still, as though in a state of erection. He stands glass in hand, bellowing. AUNT's face is covered in down, she cackles like a hen but her cackling is full of meaning: she makes speeches. From time to time everyone becomes still and the voices die away. After a few seconds everything comes to life again. The only audible words which the wedding guests call out are: 'the happy pair!'. Music. The wedding guests depart. BIANCA and BENJAMIN are sitting at the far corners of the table. They speak their monologues without paying attention to the servants who are moving the flowers and the lights on to the floor, removing the chairs and table. They bring in a big double-bed. The drawing room is changed into a bedroom. The WENCH and COOK are fussing around. They smooth the linen, arrange the pillows, sheets and coverlets. They smooth, straighten and adjust, showing things to one another in a dumb show. The lights and flowers surround the bed like a catafalque. It is not necessary to have the table removed. COOK and the WENCH can be made to arrange the mattresses, sheets, pillows and coverlets on the table. They convert the table into a double-bed, they then duck under the table, where AUNT and the others are already in hiding.

BIANCA   What did you dream, Benjamin? Your hair was sprinkled with unguents of Araby, your tunic woven from the most delicate Sidon wool. A wreath of roses on your temples and your head propped against a woman's bosom, but not of a mother or a sister, or even of your lover. Benjamin, do you understand that moment in which a woman is not yet a lover, and yet already loves and is loved? As for the woman, have you seen one that is beautiful, powerful in her sensuality, saintly in her spirit, with a forehead that is such a strength of thought that she could direct the fate of Athens, while on her lips such delight, and in her look such warm and piercing attractiveness? Have you dreamt of her? Her eyes, if lowered, are a flame only of hope or memories, they are too dazzling, and therefore are shaded, the blush on her cheek, it is life, it is blood which gushes to the outside from the bursting organism, and her love. Believe me, brother, such women there are, you may meet her and you may desire to die in her arms in order not to exist thereafter.

BENJAMIN   Give me women, wine and snuff
               Until I cry out "hold, enough!"
               You may do so sans objection
               Till the day of resurrection;
               For bless my beard they aye shall be
               My beloved trinity.
               Fill for me a brimming bowl
               And let me in it drown my soul

There is a fire in the hearth. Above the hearth a colossal mirror reflecting an uneasy moving light. The light flows through the room like a river. During BIANCA's monologue BENJAMIN has been undressing slowly but methodically. He has been doing this unnoticed, as though he wished to conceal from BIANCA these normal yet obviously improper functions. He began with the collar and cuff-links. BIANCA is lying on the bed as if in a coffin. Her eyelids are lowered but she is nevertheless watching her husband undressing. At the moment when BENJAMIN intends to pull the sock off his left foot BIANCA smiles sardonically. A shiver of disgust, of fear, shakes her.

BIANCA   Ben ... get dressed.

BENJAMIN   I love you, Bee ...

BIANCA   It's my period today, so your undressing doesn't make any sense. Don't sniff me, get dressed. Put on your trousers. (*BENJAMIN begins to dress. He even puts on his collar, etc.*) Don't touch me.

BENJAMIN sits on the edge of the bed.

BIANCA   My legs have grown together. From the feet right up to the navel I am covered in a cold fishy scale. Ben, your beloved has a fishy tail instead of legs. Do you understand? I am a siren. You've married a siren, a chimera. Look! I've got a lion's head, a goat's body and a snake's tail.

BENJAMIN   You're tired, my poor little mouse. Your paws are sweaty and damp. Are you afraid?

BIANCA   Can you hear how my sister sirens are enticing me, calling me?

BENJAMIN   I love you.

BIANCA   Lie down next to me. Don't touch me. Tell me, what do you love in me? The face, nose, lips, hair? The waist? What are you thinking about? Breasts, hams? Ben, have you ever loved? Physically? Are you asleep? Why don't you answer? Are you pretending to be asleep? (*the clock strikes the hour*) Do you remember what you promised me in the black wood? What are you thinking about now?

BENJAMIN   (*drowsy*) About you.

BIANCA   What were your thoughts when you were pulling off your trousers, your jacket, your collar?

BENJAMIN   (*mumbling*) I don't know ...

BIANCA   You do and so do I. Don't lay your head on my breasts. My armpits smell of the goat. I don't want you to sense my smell.

BENJAMIN   (*in his sleep*) Bee ... peee ... phee.

BIANCA   (*clasps her hands in prayer, touches the sleeper's lips with her lips*) Fear not, fear not. My Bennie, I won't leave you. My Bennie, I love you. You won't run away from me. I shall hold you until your hair grows white and you lose all your teeth, I'll cover you with a German duvet. I'll put a white skullcap on your head. Are you asleep, Bennie?

Light fades, silence. In the darkness something stirs: a disturbance, indistinct voices break through: 'Mariage blanc, mariage blanc, blanc ... '. Voices combine into a chorus and grow in strength.

TABLEAU 13
'I AM'

The bedroom in daylight. On the made-up bed a bunch of withering flowers. Open door to the drawing-room. Behind the door rustling of paper like someone leafing through a newspaper. BIANCA is standing in front of the hearth, looking at her image in the mirror. She is wearing a dark party dress. She adjusts her splendid hat which is like a garden full of birds and flowers. BENJAMIN's voice through the open door.

BENJAMIN   Are you ready?

BIANCA doesn't reply. She gazes into the mirror. She stretches her hands into the fire as though she wished to warm them. She looks into the fireplace for a few seconds. Motionless. Then slowly she takes off her long gloves and throws them into the fireplace. She takes her hat off and throws that into the fireplace. The buttons on her dress offer resistance, she tears the dress apart, rolls it into a ball, throws it into the fireplace. Next she gradually throws in all the items of her clothing, including her underclothes, shoes and stockings. She removes pins and combs from her hair. She stands facing the mirror naked, her hair loose. After a moment she takes a pair of long scissors and cuts off her hair close to the skin, unevenly. She puts the scissors away. She covers her breasts with her hands and speaks to her reflection in the mirror: 'I am', a moment later she cries: 'I am ready'. BENJAMIN enters the bedroom in his best suit, ready to go. He stops. BIANCA turns round slowly.

BIANCA   I am *(takes a step towards BENJAMIN)* I am ... *(slopes her shoulders)* ... your ... *(in a whisper)* brother ...

THE HUNGER ARTIST
DEPARTS

First English language production 21st August 1982, by the Oxford
Theatre Group at the Edinburgh Festival.
Directed by Ian Brunskill

THE HUNGER ARTIST ... Carl Gorham
THE IMPRESARIO ... Rick Readshaw
THE IMPRESARIO'S WIFE ... Catherine Roe
BUTCHER GUARD, MAN ... Ben Hoosen
BUTCHER GUARD, OLD BOY and FATHER ... Rolando Allen
YOUNG MOTHER, OLA and MOTHER ... Rose Cameron
BUTCHER GUARD, MAN and SMALL BOY ... Jeff Dodds
RESEARCHER, YOUNG MOTHER, MONIKA AND MOTHER ...
Ceri Sullivan

Designer ... Paul Godfrey
Lighting Director ... Mark Ager
Technical Director ... Stefan Czerniawski

THE CHARACTERS

THE HUNGER ARTIST
THE IMPRESARIO
THE IMPRESARIO'S WIFE
A YOUNG WOMAN
GUARDS
FIRST MAN
SECOND MAN
FIRST MOTHER
SECOND MOTHER
MONIKA
OLA
FATHER
SON
MOTHER
CROWD

LAUGHTER

The cage stayed shut
until a bird was hatched inside

the bird remained mute
until the cage
rusting in the silence
opened

silence lasted until
behind black wires
we heard laughter

1: PROLOGUE — A SHORT TREATISE ON HUNGER ARTISTS

For several years now I have been circling round the Hunger Artist. The circles are growing smaller, tighter. Sometimes I get the feeling that I have caught, imprisoned and immobilised my 'hero', only to realize that, once more, he has slipped out and moved away. I first came across this short story in 1956. The little volume lies here on the table with lines scored at various times in red, black and green. The Hunger Artist (underlined in red) *'bleich, im schwarzen Trikot'*. All the while I felt a sense of deprivation, anxiety and fear. Not a fear of 'critics', but a fear of Franz K.: what use is my goodwill and the skill which I had acquired in my struggles with the theatre and drama over twenty years?

Franz K. was the authentic *Hungerkünstler*; he was slim and emaciated. With his appearance he scared away — tried to scare away — wretched 'fiancées', candidates pressing for the Hunger Artist's hand. He himself admired fatties, felt sympathetic towards the fat Franz Werfel. Stayed awake at night. What did he eat? Neither the diaries nor the letters provide clear information on this score. A Hunger Artist. I had noticed that the Hunger Artist knows nothing and doesn't want to know anything about the existence of other hunger artists. He lives as though he were the only Hunger Artist on earth. His only interest is his hunger. In fact, he has no interests. Even the Great War takes place on the periphery of his life, the real war takes place in his body. Fat, normal, healthy young bourgeois sirens tempt him with their song. But nest-building (the family-hearth) stirs him into panic. Couple. Coupling. Couplet. That amuses and terrifies him. He partakes of the unique and the chosen. It seems to me that bringing other hunger artists into the body of the play (I employed the Impresario for that purpose) was justified, although I do realize that this was a painful move for the hunger artist. The very possibility of the existence of other hunger artists is intolerable and offensive. The Hunger Artist does not react to the Impresario's words when he describes the existence of new hunger artists more adapted to our times. We ordinary bread-eaters find it hard to imagine the shock felt by the Hunger Artist at the arrival on the scene of another hunger artist. What a shock for the authentic 'chosen' Hunger Artist are posters, photographs and interviews with new numerous hunger artists. And what does it mean for the Hunger Artist to be confronted with another, equally distinguished but more popular, more 'worldly' hunger artist? Naturally, our Hunger Artist (the unique and chosen) will never, never, acknowledge in his heart of hearts the existence of another hunger artist who is his equal in everything, including privations and sins. Were he to acquiesce, he would immediately break off his fast, tear up his agreement with the Impresario, go into a desert and die conscious of the fact that the other hunger artist (equally great, although this would be the public's delusion) is nevertheless a worse hunger artist because he lives admired, breaks off his fasts and, in moments free from fasting, accepts food and perhaps even turns into a gourmet! Let us not be too cruel to the real Hunger Artist, let us not be too cruel to the numerous, constantly increasing numbers of false hunger artists.

2: CONVERSATION WITH THE HUNGER ARTIST

THE HUNGER ARTIST and a YOUNG WOMAN sit on a bench in front of the curtain.

YOUNG WOMAN   Why do you fast? How did you hit on this idea, how did it all start? When you fast, do you regard yourself as better than those who eat sensibly, or even gorge themselves?

HUNGER ARTIST   No, I fast for them; for those who are well-fed. My fasting only makes sense amongst well-fed people. Fasting amongst those dying of hunger, that's surely a nonsense. At times I feel contempt for those over there. Look, those are the guardians of my fast. They are professional butchers. They eat and drink with breaks for work, sleep and sex. But I immediately stifle those nasty feelings. For it is those who eat, those who consume that support the structure of our contemporary civilisation. And if it weren't for their indulgence, everything might have collapsed. So I fast for them.

YOUNG WOMAN   And what's your attitude to other hunger artists?

HUNGER ARTIST   So you think there are others? Ah well, it's not a subject I like to discuss and in any case I have no friendly outgoing feelings. Well, there is a certain curiosity. I am suspicious of contemporary hunger artists. The true great Hunger Artist is the classical dead Hunger Artist. Things have gone on so far they are now setting up clubs for hunger artists with an ordinary chairman, secretary and treasurer. Associations of young hunger artists and of aspiring hunger artists are multiplying.

YOUNG WOMAN   Do your feelings spring from a natural, professional dislike, from fear of competitions, or do you, knowing yourself, feel distrustful towards other hunger artists?

HUNGER ARTIST   You've raised several matters, for example the question of professional antipathy. True, the sham hunger artists cover it up very carefully, they make bitter-sweet faces at everything. Since they are themselves inauthentic, it's easy for them to love and admire similar beings, but they hate the real Hunger Artist. True, no one, of course, can live absolutely alone. It's the same even with gods, prophets and messiahs. Even they possess this childish ambition, they wish to be unique and unrepeatable: the chosen. It's the same with showmen and hunger artists, even the most paltry and silliest hunger artist nourishes a vision of his uniqueness and originality. Imagine forty hunger artists in my cage. Or better still don't!

YOUNG WOMAN   But let's get back to you. The cage is a symbol of enslavement: a lion in a cage, an eagle in a cage ...

HUNGER ARTIST   In choosing a cage I chose freedom: a freedom totally unrestricted by either tradition or authority or conventions or ... but even this business of the cage isn't simple. You see, 'the cage as such' has no meaning. An empty cage may be shut or open. An empty cage isn't even a cage. Only that which is inside the cage which is locked up in the cage gives it a meaning and even dignity. And now, back to me in my cage. Imagine that someone has thrown you inside without reason, without a verdict. For you and your nearest and dearest this means violence, cruelty and lawlessness. You are deprived of freedom, of that which is holiest and irreplaceable, guaranteed by 'a general declaration of human rights', and so on and so on. But I feel good in the cage and have made the most of my freedom there. I've retained a freedom of choice. I chose the cage and therefore I am free in the cage. My freedom is more real than the freedom of my guards, the citizens of this town, and yours as well. But I do not wish to analyze this phenomenon too deeply in case I turn into an academic, nor am I trying to persuade anyone to follow in my footsteps – the hunger artist's profession.

YOUNG WOMAN   Profession! Did you say 'profession'?!

HUNGER ARTIST   You are quick, but don't catch me out over words.

YOUNG WOMAN   So what can I catch you at? You are surely ...?

HUNGER ARTIST Let's leave aside these Różewicz-type jokes! So you caught me at the word 'profession'. I don't wish to make excuses. I'm no longer an amateur. I am a professional Hunger Artist. Picasso is a professional painter. Jarocki is a professional theatre director. We also have professional cardinals, philosophers, actors. Only failed poets shudder at the sound of this word. But enough said ... even saints are professionals.

YOUNG WOMAN From your earlier reply I conclude you take no interest in imitators, pupils or followers.

HUNGER ARTIST If I could, I would chase them away with a stick. Locked in a cage, I promise no one transfiguration, liberation, salvation or parturition. I am sitting in a cage, and when they stare at me, I want people to become aware of their misery but that at the same time they should somehow have fun at my expense and also enjoy themselves. I don't nourish pseudo-mystical hungers, nor do I arouse them in the younger generation. Don't hang about. There is no mystery and there won't be any.

3: NIGHT WATCHING

Spotlight on a group of BUTCHER-GUARDS. These GUARDS play an important role in the play. They must be drawn into the action and allowed to speak. Kafka didn't put a single word in their mouths. Their job is to see that, day or night, THE HUNGER ARTIST doesn't obtain food in any underhand way. The GUARDs' role is in fact only a show created for the public. Those in the know are aware that during a fast THE HUNGER ARTIST does not receive food under any pretext, nor even under pressure, die Ehre seiner Kunst verbot dies. Some GUARDS perform their duties in a deliberately casual manner, they sit in a distant corner and become totally absorbed in a game of cards, as if they wanted THE HUNGER ARTIST to have a little snack. Such behaviour would particularly depress THE HUNGER ARTIST, making his fast especially difficult. He would then overcome his weakness and sing day and night, in order to demonstrate to these men that their suspicions and behaviour were unjust and hurtful. But this was no use. The thick-skinned crowd only marvelled at the cunning devil who could eat and sing at the same time. Everything arouses suspicion because THE HUNGER ARTIST himself is 'suspect'.

Forty days: that was the limit. THE IMPRESARIO wouldn't allow him to cross this boundary as the public's interest would then wane instead of increasing. THE HUNGER ARTIST would hint and even beg the Impresario to extend the fast, but would meet with categorical refusal. But why forty days, rather than thirty-three or forty-four? Perhaps THE IMPRESARIO had once read that 'Jesus, being full of the Holy Ghost, returned from Jordan, and was led by the Spirit into the wilderness, being forty days tempted of the devil. And in those days he did eat nothing. And when they were ended, he afterwards hungered.'

THE GUARDS sit at a table shaped like a tree-trunk. Glasses of light ale, sausages and rolls. Around the table a few empty bottles, papers and empty tins. The cage stands in darkness beyond the spotlight. It's shape is blurred, almost invisible, occasionally perhaps its metal bars may catch the light. They eat and drink in silence, belching from time to time. They are now drowsy and tired. The clock strikes with a beautiful clear sound as if it came from another world. It's three o'clock. The beam of light which fell on the GUARDs' table grows dim. In the *silence a song. It's THE HUNGER ARTIST singing. The melody is vigorous, almost bouncy, and the childish words resound in the unawakened space, as though THE HUNGER ARTIST were trying to demonstrate the absurdity and unreality of the world.*

HUNGER ARTIST   (*sings*)   Poor Rover from the kitchen slab
        Did steal some juicy meat,
        A cruel stupid cook went mad
        And killed him for this feat.

THE GUARDS listen. One of them gets up, kicks an empty tin, goes towards the darkness and stops as though peeing. He approaches the cage. The bars of the cage now appear a little more clearly, but the inside of the cage is still plunged in soot-like darkness. All the while THE HUNGER ARTIST sings his song. THE GUARD stands for a while, his hands and face touching the cage bars, then he returns to the table. He sits heavily on a small folding chair.

GUARD 1   Sod ... Keeps awake, won't let others sleep ...

Throws an empty bottle at the cage, the sound of breaking glass. The singing stops.

GUARD 2 (*catching THE FIRST GUARD by the arm*) Jesus Christ, you
        could have killed him!

GUARD 1   Bugger off or I'll spit in your eyes!

They struggle. GUARD 3 sleeps, his head propped on the table. He raises his head for a moment, looks around blearily and falls asleep again.

GUARD 2   You volunteered, nobody forced you to.

GUARD 1   Well, I wanted to catch him at it. The sod, pulling wool
        over my eyes. He must be stuffing himself silly. I really get mad —
        the cunning bastard!

GUARD 2   You're out of your mind, we guard him in turn and he sings
        all night. Can't you see? When he sings he can't stuff himself.

GUARD 1   Son of a bitch that can stuff himself and sing.

GUARD 2   Oh, you clever sod, singing isn't like farting, you know.

THE GUARDS clink their glasses and drink beer. They mumble drowsily and fall asleep. The light over the table grows dim, the contours and faces of the sleepers turn yellow and violet, while the light around the cage begins to pierce through the darkness, weaving the shape of the cage and its interior. The cage may resemble an old-fashioned budgerigar cage (but this is of no great importance) or it may resemble

81

an ape's cage in a menagerie with bars made of nylon or string or shining rods. The floor of the cage has wooden boards, on them a pile of straw covered with a grey blanket. There is also a bucket and a glass of water. A clock. The cage door is padlocked. Above the door, a blackboard with a chalked '33'. It's the thirty-third 24-hour period of the fast. Every morning, THE IMPRESARIO personally chalks up the successive figure.

4:   THE HUNGER ARTIST WAKES

The shape under the blanket resembles a human being. The blanket stirs, the straw rustles. White hands poke out, then a face. The hands gesticulate wildly. THE HUNGER ARTIST sits up with an outstretched fist. Moves his lips towards the hand and speaks.

HUNGER ARTIST   Greetings sister fly
          you tiny creature
          alighting on my nose
          you've woken me to life
          you buzz begging for freedom
          be carefree
          fly your way
          there a choir of your sisters
          now welcomes the dawn
          the sun from the hills
          steps in a procession
          of your pestilential tribe
          away away fly
          stirring life
          in god's corpse
          (*slowly THE HUNGER ARTIST opens his palm, examines it and puts his ear to it*) The fly is dead. What have I done to you my sister fly. Are we humans not merely flies in the hands of gods? It's they who pull out our feet and wings. They shut up our imperfect bodies in bottles and feed us with mystical crumbs. Ah me! A poor human fly without wings, who will hear my buzz in this our bottle called the universe, the globe.
          You lie dead in my palm
          black lifeless soulless
          I took your life
          but who gave you life
          a conscience stick
          is breaking my back

I am not the brother of the fly
I torture it and let it die

We sinners admire only the swarming bees, we praise the sacred busy bees because they give us honey. Oh, sister-flies, is it your fault that your disgusting parasitic species doesn't collect honey for us? Forgive us, flies, and you, spirits of murdered flies. My poor little fly, I shall arrange a funeral, I'll bury you inside a straw, in a split between the floor-boards.

A bass voice emerges from the bushes

IMPRESARIO   (*sings*) The shining sun
Is warming the land
Paper in hand
I go to sh ... ining sun
Is warming the land ...

THE IMPRESSARIO emerges onto the path, holding a newspaper. He is a huge, monstrously fat man. He may be stuffed or pumped up in a rubber suit like the Michelin man. A huge red friendly mug.

IMPRESARIO   Good morning. And how are we today, maestro? what's all this lamentation over a dead fly? I've never heard such a rich stream of rhetoric from your lips, maestro. Human corpses don't move you, maestro. 'Fly, my sister ... My little fly ... I've killed a living being ... I've taken your life ... bla bla bla'. Why do you stare at me in this oafish way? Have you never seen a human being, maestro?

GUARD 1   (*waking up with a cry*) Stop! Who goes there?!

IMPRESARIO   I thank you in the name of duty. Flies are shitting, spring is coming!

GUARD 1   (*shaking GUARD 2*) Wake up! Wake up! Réveillé!!!

GUARD 2   What? Where ... where?

GUARD 1   Go grab him! The Hunger Artist has snatched your sausage! After him!

GUARD 3   (*stretching and yawning*) You keep watch, I'll fetch breakfast (*goes away*)

IMPRESARIO   Maestro, I brought you the morning paper still smelling of printer's ink.

Stretches his hand to pass the paper to THE HUNGER ARTIST. THE HUNGER ARTIST *shakes his head in refusal and turns his back to* THE IMPRESARIO *and presses a clenched fist against his ear.*

IMPRESARIO (*passing the newspaper to* THE GUARD) Read it, gentlemen! And you too should listen, there's a really expert article on flies, no mamby-pamby stuff. (*departs singing*)
The shining sun
Is warming the land
Paper in hand
I go to sh … ining sun
Is warming the land …

GUARD 3 *returns with a sack full of bones and a bowl full of raw meat. Pulls the bones out of the sack, breaks them up with a chopper and sucks the marrow. The other two eat the meat with their hands, straight from the bowl. They break off, wiping their hands with the newspaper.*

GUARD 1 (*smoothes out the newspaper and begins to read silently, breaks off*) This is about flies. The manager said we are to read aloud to Mr Hunger Artist because he himself doesn't want to read it. He despises the press.

GUARD 2 And what is it about?

GUARD 1 Flies.

GUARD 2 Flies? He's eaten a fly?

GUARD 1 That I don't know, but he's killed one and now he's weeping over her body.

GUARD 2 You're nuts. Killed a fly and cries?

GUARD 1 He's not the first, there was an ancient saint, a doctor, who killed a bed-bug, then spent two years crying over himself and the bug. He prayed to the Almighty and begged forgiveness …

GUARD 2 Killed a bug? A saintly doctor? An academic?

GUARD 1 A bug or maybe a louse, I don't remember.

GUARD 2 You've got it wrong. It was a rabbi who killed a louse. He didn't cry. 'An eye for an eye, a tooth for a tooth,' you know.

GUARD 3 (*stops sucking the bone, listens to the conversation, butts in*) Well, old man, in my time I've killed a hundred ox, a hundred cows, a thousand calves and some two thousand pigs and he slobbers over a fly. You have a hundred of them dancing under a pig's tail. We are supposed to be the murderers while various holy men weep and stuff themselves as much as they can. Crying over a fly ... the weed, he's never seen how sad cows and pigs are. I think pigs are the most sensitive, they know they are going to die. They are sad, old man. For Chrissake, I've seen them cry. They lose weight. ... we were losing so much meat, the Institute looked into it. They started giving pigs tranquilising injections.

GUARD 2   Come off it!

GUARD 3   Don't you read the press? The injections worked. The pigs calmed down and went to slaughter self-possessed. They even gained in weight, although they were a little apathetic and indifferent, but although there was more meat, they had to stop the practice because they discovered that in our canton people were going crazy suffering from strange mental disorders. The experts at the Institute discovered that these symptoms appeared in people who regularly had been eating the meat of pigs that were tranquilized with injections. All of these are facts, scientific facts, old man!

GUARD 2   The world is full of wonders. The greatest swine hasn't even dreamt of them.

GUARD 2 and GUARD 3 are lost in thought, eating the meat out of the bowl.

GUARD 1   (*reading aloud*) 'For already in ancient Greece flies constituted a real plague in the summer season and the annual ox sacrifice was intended to kindle mercy for suffering mankind. And long before the Greeks, the ancient Syrians also offered bloody sacrifices to the housefly, from which it appears that the fly is indeed an eternal plague of mankind.'

The clock strikes eight. GUARD 1 and GUARD 2 leave. GUARD 3 stays behind by the tree-trunk table at which THE BUTCHER-GUARDS had just been eating.

5: IN THE LIGHT OF DAY

THE HUNGER ARTIST's cage is on a stand. At the back, a small 'concert bowl' and a small shed bearing the notice 'Box Office'. The stand is roped off. A park path runs nearby. A green lawn. In the distance a few trees. Paths covered in gravel. The tree-trunk table and chairs stand not far from the cage. A young plump attractive woman emerges from the shed. She is carrying a bowl with multi-coloured washing. Under her arm she is carrying a bundle of white rope. She ties the line between the shed and THE HUNGER ARTIST's cage. She is hanging out men's and ladies' underwear which she secures with clothes pegs. THE GUARDS are talking, occasionally bursting into laughter, telling each other political and dirty jokes. THE WOMAN has finished hanging out the washing, lingers by the cage and then, without a word, goes back to the shed and reappears in the window of the shed marked 'Box Office'.

Various people are seen running along the path at 30-second intervals: an elderly, white-haired well-fed man in a blue track suit (he reappears three times, each time his breathing and movements are different) who is followed by two young women in vests and shorts. The path is perhaps part of the park's health area. THE IMPRESARIO comes out of the shed, walks over to the cage, rubs out the figure '33' and chalks in '34'. Peers into the cage. He turns into the shed and his head reappears next to the woman's head at the window. Two middle-aged men dressed in expensive sheep-skin coats and fur caps (although it's now May) sit down on the bench. Their dialogue is a continuation of a dialogue they were having in the real world before they came on stage.

FIRST MAN ... or just a wholesome smoked sausage, with fat under the skin. But no mustard, only horse-raddish.

SECOND MAN Or perhaps ox tongue.

FIRST MAN A beetroot soup with barley, don't you think? A Lithuanian beetroot soup, a slice of bacon or perhaps a sausage.

SECOND MAN A duckling's leg with beetroots and a sauce. Sour cream and plenty of wind.

FIRST MAN Sour cream, potatoes in meat sauce, bacon, peas and a splendid fart.

SECOND MAN Pig's knuckle with peas is also recommended.

FIRST MAN Trotters with bacon.

SECOND MAN With fat and chilled vodka – neat.

FIRST MAN Eels are also good with vodka in a carafe.

SECOND MAN Meat *à la tartare* with thinly sliced onion and egg yolk and a suitable garnish. A drop of vinegar, a little bread, black pudding but with liver and mustard.

FIRST MAN Whatever you say, I wouldn't mind *escallopes à la hongroise*.

SECOND MAN They say they bought up several tons of frozen meat.

FIRST MAN It's goulash today.

SECOND MAN You should have seen their tasty fried risotto and cabbage.

The men get up and go. Two young MOTHERS pushing prams come along the path. Twins in one, in the other triplets or perhaps quintuplets. THE MOTHERS sit on the bench, spreading out shopping bags and baskets, they adjust the children's blankets and chat, both turned towards the audience.

MOTHER I Every mother's greatest wish is the health and proper development of her child.

MOTHER II What should a child aged 1 to 3 be consuming daily?

MOTHER I Many young mums make mistakes due to wrongly conceived care. They overfeed their darlings with sweets and other foods they themselves like, most often at the expense of the most valuable nutriments such as milk, cheese, fruit and vegetables.

MOTHER II Which leads to excessive obesity.

MOTHER I The tiny tots ought to consume the following foodstuffs daily:
a variety of bread – 4 oz
flour and macaroni – 1 oz
porridge – 1 oz
.milk – 18 oz
cream cheese – 1 oz

curd cheese – $\frac{1}{4}$ oz

AN OLD BOY shuffles up to the bench. He raises his hat and sits on the edge of the bench. Unfolds a newspaper and reads aloud.

OLD BOY 'India takes drastic steps in a fight against her demographic explosion. The government of West Bengal, a province inhabited by 50 million people, intends to bring a law providing that couples with three or more children must, on pain of a penalty or imprisonment, submit to sterilization.'

MOTHER I
    meat – 1 oz
    sausages – $\frac{1}{4}$ oz
    butter – $\frac{1}{4}$ oz
    cream – $\frac{1}{4}$ oz
    other fats – $\frac{1}{8}$ oz

OLD BOY 'The authorities in Delhi, India's capital with five million inhabitants, had already announced in February that government workers and private individuals having two or more children will not be able to benefit from free medical care, will not be allowed to change their jobs, negotiate bank loans, accommodation and other facilities, if they don't submit to sterilization ...'

MOTHER II What a callous doddery swine! In front of women and little children, how dare he!

MOTHER I
    sugar – 1 oz
    jam and marmalade – $\frac{1}{4}$ oz
    carotene vegetables – 5 oz
    other vegetables – 5 oz

OLD BOY 'However, the population of India, which now numbers 605 million, is increasing monthly by one million and before the end of the century will reach a billion. In West Bengal, whose government intends to introduce the most drastic measures, there are about 570 people per square kilometre, in other words, five times more than in Poland.'

MOTHER II And they stay alive all those years. They ought to round them up. The country is full of unnatural deviants and what's the police doing about it?

MOTHER I   Don't pay any attention. A repulsive old reptile. I am sure he isn't Polish, must be German or Czech.

MOTHER II   He can't be Czech, just look at that snout. Observe how he stares ... a typical Turk!

MOTHER I   Probably a Jehovah's Witness or a communist or a Jew. Not a Catholic.

MOTHER II   Only a beast would say things like that in front of women and children. (*shouting*) Shame! You old hog!

THE OLD BOY terrified runs away into the bushes. THE MOTHERS adjust the blankets and full of dignity push prams laden with fruits of love.

6: EVENING COMES

Gas lamps light up amongst the trees. On a bench a young couple fondle and kiss hungrily and passionately, in silence. THE IMPRESARIO stands next to the box-office, his WIFE's head is at the window. The cage with THE HUNGER ARTIST and the barely visible GUARDS' table plunged in darkness.

IMPRESARIO What's the taking like?

WIFE Twenty crowns.

IMPRESARIO It's worse and worse, won't even be enough for food soon.

WIFE Surely, you have nothing against Ernest. He really doesn't eat.

IMPRESARIO And he does nothing else, either. Just sits in a corner, fasts and waits for the applause and thinks nothing's changed. '*Es waren andere Zeiten*'. Passive fasting was good enough before the war, now you have to fast actively, even aggressively. I myself am having doubts about the sense of the whole show. Just between us, I've had enough of his arrogance. The great wonder 'doesn't eat' with his nose up in the air ...

WIFE But he doesn't talk. He's submissive, doesn't complain.

IMPRESARIO Precisely. Doesn't complain, doesn't talk, but that's due to conceit, not humility. I know a thing or two about these artist-gentlemen, these conjurors, these Jesuits. (*sneering*) A great artist. A *Hungerkünstler*. If it goes on like this, we won't be eating either what with the upkeep, taxes, advertising, the devaluation of the crown. Even keeping the cage tidy costs money.

WIFE I clean the cage myself and I don't get the impression you pay me anything extra for it. The guards don't take a penny. Ernest costs us as much as a little sparrow. In forty days he drinks two or three glasses of water and he does it with great restraint. In fact, he doesn't drink at all. He just moistens his lips and tongue.

IMPRESARIO   He isn't human. He's vermin.

WIFE   He is human.

IMPRESARIO   You like him, you prefer him to me. You should have waited until he proposed to you. (*WIFE shrugs her shoulders*) I'm not blind. You neglect me and the home. Instead of cooking something tasty and nourishing, you walk around the cage in admiration, with a glazed look fixed on him. When Arthur died I should have got another monkey but the devil tempted me to burden myself with this sponger. But God help you, if you two give me horns I'll cut off his head or his balls against this tree-trunk. What's this cow-like stare? Let's have something edible for dinner for a change. He doesn't need looking after like a baby. You don't have to change his nappies. He doesn't wet them. He can't.

WIFE   While you shit enough for two.

IMPRESARIO   Why don't you lock yourself up in that cage and fast with him?

WIFE   Perhaps …

IMPRESARIO   Bla, bla, bla. So long … I'm off to see the mayor. He's got to be invited to the ceremony. (*pats WIFE on the head*) You're stupid, you're forty and you behave like a teenager. Any minute now you'll start writing verses. The butchers were saying they were slaughtering pigs. Tomorrow we'll have blood-sausage and brawn. Don't forget, I'll repay you in bed.

THE IMPRESARIO walks away along the path. THE WIFE takes down the washing, folds it and goes away. In the dim light THE GUARDS can be seen playing cards, calling out words and phrases suited to the game. THE HUNGER ARTIST sits with his head bowed. Only his head is picked out by the spotlight. THE WIFE stands in the darkness, motionless. Slowly, she moves towards the cage, her arms straight against her body. Now the light falls on her. THE HUNGER ARTIST opens his eyes, looks silently at THE WIFE, then closes his eyes. THE WIFE adjusts her coiffure, binds her hair together with pins she's been gripping between her teeth, she fixes her hair and smiles at THE HUNGER ARTIST. But it's only a shadow of a smile, which passes. THE WIFE stands undecided, straightens her dress, is on the point of saying something (maybe she mumbles the word 'I') then turns round and goes away. THE HUNGER ARTIST takes no notice of her. The spotlight now moves towards THE

GUARDS. *The cage is in darkness. From the darkness comes a quiet uncertain song. Soon we can distinguish its words*:

HUNGER ARTIST   Poor Rover from the kitchen slab
    Did steal some juicy meat
    A cruel stupid cook went mad
    And killed him for this feat

    Another much more kindly cook
    Who Rover's slaughter saw

GUARDS   (*break off the game and bawl*)

    Set up a splendid tombstone there
    Which this inscription bore:

GUARD 1   (*to HUNGER ARTIST*) God Almighty! The little woman is all sugar and spice. She sighs, she pines … and you? Aren't you ashamed? You count flies, you catch them and slobber, you munch straw …

GUARD 2   She's a rare bird. If only she came my way, poor little woman. She preens herself and wiggles her bottom. There is no go in you, maestro!

GUARD 3 (*yawning and stretching*) I'll have some shut-eye. You guard him.

GUARD 1   There is nothing to guard! The gentleman has his honour! Not like you, just wanting to stuff your belly and lay a bird. (*turning to THE HUNGER ARTIST*) Mr Hunger Artist, take a lead from my colleague and have a nap.

HUNGER ARTIST   I don't need sleep.

GUARD 2   There is a lucky man for you. Doesn't eat, doesn't drink. You can't fault that!

THE GUARDS *continue to play cards in complete silence. Their gestures are conventional, the only sound is that of the cards. Their silence lasts about 10 seconds. A thin strip of light now lingers on the face, or rather just the black-painted lips, of THE HUNGER ARTIST.*

HUNGER ARTIST   I speak to you,
    night
    I'm free in this cage
    I speak to the stars, to silence

three steps forward
three steps back
I have enough room
to stretch my arms
I'm free
like the air.

(*THE HUNGER ARTIST changes his 'delivery', continuing in an ordinary matter-of-fact voice*) I sit here of my own free will. Only from what the Guards say do I learn where I am but that doesn't interest me. In Radomsko, Paris, Piotrków*, Rome, Venice and Wrocław*, in Bombay and Berlin, all that interests me is my hunger. But even that doesn't interest me. After forty days, when the Impressario breaks my fast, when they open the cage, when two choice maidens lead me to a table set with rare dishes, I'm filled with anger and fury. I can go on fasting for another forty days but the Impresario is arranging the opening ceremony. When all these revolting celebrations are over, I can leave the cage. My best suit, still quite decent, awaits me. I can go to the barber, I can order a masseuse and refreshed I can go to see the sights, the fashion houses, theatres and editorial offices.

I used to do this regularly
after every fast
but now I don't make use of these opportunities
I feel no need
to visit coffee houses and restaurants
I keep my salary next to my heart
I can spend it in an hour
but I have no needs

my only interest is fasting
and even that I have to break off in the most absorbing moment
I remember a conversation I once had with a certain academic
I was young then
I imagined that fasting was an achievement
that it was something extraordinary and deserving admiration
that it entitled me to certain privileges
they even handed me awards and diplomas
I joined the HUNGER ARTISTS' CLUB

* Note: pronounced Piotrkoov and Vrotzwav respectively.

I ate tasty and cheap lunches
at the HUNGER ARTISTS' canteen
I took part in a number
of HUNGER ARTISTS' concerts and festivals
I then left for the provinces
I hid away for twenty years in a cave
I began to understand the difference between real fasting
and 'wordly' fasting
I was breaking the ties.

7: NIGHT COMES

THE HUNGER ARTIST lies down in the straw and pulls up the blanket. Light above the cage fades. The clock strikes twelve. Midnight. THE IMPRESARIO's WIFE emerges from the darkness. She carries a jug of water, a towel and a bowl. She comes up to THE GUARDS. They are sprawled on the ground around the cage. THE WIFE comes close to the cage, gazes at THE HUNGER ARTIST for a moment, then sits down by the tree-trunk table.

WIFE   They sleep ... they sleep. They are all asleep. My husband replete with beer and pig's knuckle, sleeps embracing the air or the pillow and thinks it's my body. The guards replete with blood-sausage and lager sleep instead of watching over the Hunger Artist's fast. And the Hunger Artist sleeps on an empty stomach. The park sleeps. The town sleeps. The gold coin sleeps in the box office. No one counts it, no one checks it, no one touches it.

The spotlight now moves towards THE HUNGER ARTIST's cage. In the faint light THE WIFE takes off her shirt, washes her arms, her breasts and neck, puts the bowl on the ground and washes her feet. Now THE WIFE's voice emerges from the darkness. As if the darkness were talking to THE HUNGER ARTIST.

WIFE   Come to me
        I want to be with you
        says the deep night
        I know you are not asleep
        give me a sign
        I'll rush towards you
        my body yearns for you and desires you
        give me a sign
        why do you push me away
        why do you push away life
        you see me whole I have unveiled myself before you
        I know there is no woman in your life

I want to sleep with you
with your hunger
with the fire which consumes your body
I'll nourish you with my tongue
my saliva
as children do
with a chick fallen out of a nest
I want nothing from you
I only want you
in all these long years
you only once saw me
as a woman
I touched your little hand
only once or twice
those fragile tiny bones covered with skin
where do you get this strength
the town sleeps while you watch
the guards sleep while you watch

Slowly THE WIFE emerges from the darkness and comes close to the cage.

but I know you are not asleep
I have the key give me a sign
that you'll let me in
I want to come into you
I have the key

THE WIFE presses her face against the bars of the cage

I know you're not asleep
you don't want me you despise my body

THE WIFE opens the cage and enters. She stands motionless over THE HUNGER ARTIST.

My body disgusts you
you despise me

She kneels next to THE HUNGER ARTIST and takes his hand. He doesn't react and remains silent.

your hand is as light
as a wing
my breasts and thighs

yearn for your hands
my lips

*THE HUNGER ARTIST turns his face towards THE WIFE. His eyes are
closed. His face appears cut off from the body covered in a black leotard.*

you push me away
you evacuate me I know you see
with the eyes of the imagination
how we have intercourse
two wretched animals whose entrails
are filled with the meat
of other animals
I swear to you that for a week
he has neither mounted nor touched me
I wished to come to you purified
in body and in thought
I am clean
I applied every ruse
to stop him having me
I lied I said I was ill
once I had to lie beneath him
as you know we have only one bed
I was with him
I was alone

*The light is on THE HUNGER ARTIST's face. His lips are moving as if he
wished to express and shape a word. His lips part. THE HUNGER ARTIST
lies with his lips open. The light leaves the cage, wandering unsure around the
stage and the audience, as if looking for a place to stop. For a moment it lights up
the face of a spectator, then returns to the cage. THE WIFE is sitting on the
bedding, holding THE HUNGER ARTIST's head on her bosom, she leans over
him.*

You are helpless like a baby
like a child
I shall never bear
are you dead?
but your heart is beating

She touches THE HUNGER ARTIST's breast with her hand:

it beats in that wretched breast cage
closed by you

your heart beats stronger
faster under my palm
it beats for me
the heart speaks to me
the wretched and dumb
muscle
tells me you are alive
desiring my body
desiring a woman

take me

*The clock strikes a night hour. Dumb and motionless, THE HUNGER
ARTIST lies on THE WIFE's breast.*

I never felt my body
created from top to toe
from lip to mouth by the gentle
hand of a lover
I have been a mattress
and a vessel full of impurities
I have been a machine for producing
delight an instrument for erotic
exercises
and yet I am a vessel
created to receive love

*Slowly, with deliberation, pausing, THE WIFE unbuttons her white blouse.
There should be at least 12 buttons — this is to do with the rhythm, not the buttons.
She shells a beautiful heavy breast.*

you are hungry
I'll feed you

*With the pink nipple she touches the black line of THE HUNGER ARTIST's
lips, with feather-like gentleness she caresses his burnt lips.*

open, unclench ...

*She tries to push her nipple into THE HUNGER ARTIST's mouth. He turns
his head away. At that moment there is a powerful burst of savage laughter.
Squealing and croaking. It is THE BUTCHER-GUARDS. They have been
pretending to be asleep. They had spied on and heard the whole scene between
THE HUNGER ARTIST and THE IMPRESARIO's WIFE. Total
darkness. Laughter grows and continues in the darkness for at least 30 seconds.*

8:   YET ANOTHER DAY

A sunny day. THE HUNGER ARTIST is sitting in the straw. THE WIFE's head is visible at the window. She is carefully groomed and painted. Two girls sitting at the table. School uniforms. White collars. They are weaving garlands out of green shoots embellished with colourful flowers. One of the cage bars is already decorated with a garland. IMPRESARIO appears, stops: smiling, pats the girls on their heads and gives them lollies. The girls express their thanks in unison and return to their work with renewed vigour. THE IMPRESARIO goes to the cage and writes '39' on the board, pulls out a cigarette case, offers it to THE HUNGER ARTIST, together with a lighted match. They smoke in silence, then converse, but their voices are inaudible. Slowly, at intervals, members of the brass band, some five or six men and a conductor, begin to assemble on the stand. They chat and try out their instruments. Characters from scene 5 reappear along the health path, dressed as previously, running and jogging along at set intervals. THE GUARDS are standing by the box-office, chatting to THE IMPRESARIO's WIFE. There are now only two of them, the third has joined the band. The girls walk fast, they chatter indistinctly, OLA sticks her tongue out at all the adults behind their backs.

OLA   They're opening the cage tomorrow, with all the fun. I'm terribly pleased we shall be appearing. But will he last till tomorrow?

MONICA   Mum's sewn me a new dress, it's long powder-blue satin. All the girls will be green with envy.

OLA   Forty days. I think he must nibble things at night.

MONICA   At night the guards watch him in turn. They check the seals.

OLA   I'm sure they cheat.

MONICA   Shshshshsh. He'll hear you. You know what? Yesterday, I stood for an hour outside the cage, he didn't move, he never looked at me. I thought he died and I ran away.

OLA   It's now 39 days since he's stopped eating.

THE IMPRESARIO moves away towards the box-office, talks to THE GUARDS.

OLA   He's smoking a cigarette. Do you think that's allowed? Perhaps we ought to report him.

MONICA   He's looking at us. How sad he is!

OLA   Sad! you try not eating for 39 days. For three days, one day. When I was still a child I wanted to become a saint and I fasted the whole of Good Friday. All I had was a glass of tea and a rusk and by lunchtime I was so sad even the adults were looking at me with respect. And in the kitchen granny called me 'our little saint'. I was so mad I could have kicked her, that's how hungry I was. It must be the same with him.

MONICA   My daddy too is a practising believer. When he fasts on Fridays all he eats is a herring, a little fish, scrambled eggs, a few mushrooms, cucumbers and eggs in mayonnaise. He spends the whole day making himself a nuisance in the kitchen. Once I caught him eating a chunk of garlic sausage.

OLA   I've never had garlic sausage but I do know the dry steamed sausage and it isn't as tasty as it used to be before the war when my daddy got a medal because he fought.

MONICA   My daddy has two medals.

OLA   Poor little Hunger Artist! He looks so terrible, I hope he won't kick the bucket before tomorrow.

MONICA   Daddy said he earns more than managers of traditional, commercial theatres do.

OLA   A bit of a drip.

MONICA   I'm telling you, he does nibble. I've some nuts here for the squirrels. Nuts are very nourishing. Hope the guards won't see. Here, you throw them in.

THE GIRLS approach the cage on tiptoe.

OLA   (*throws a nut into the cage*) Sir, do you know that tomorrow we shall lead you out of the cage with full ceremony? Please eat. The guards aren't looking.

MONICA   Nuts are very nourishing.

His back turned, THE HUNGER ARTIST takes no notice.

MONICA   Don't cry, sir. They are preparing an excellent little something for tomorrow. The best cook is getting ready light refreshments, as though you were his dearest convalescent.

OLA sticks her tongue out at THE HUNGER ARTIST. THE HUNGER ARTIST turns round and OLA curtsies beautifully. Now, for the first time, THE HUNGER ARTIST smiles, or rather grimaces, shows his teeth. THE GIRLS are a little frightened. They step back.

HUNGER ARTIST   What are these garlands you are weaving, children? For whom ...

OLA   Guess.

HUNGER ARTIST   Is it for the sacred cow? Or to welcome a bishop?

OLA   An ass, more likely.

MONICA   (*nudges OLA*) How could you?!

HUNGER ARTIST   You laugh at me? I'm very glad you laugh openly. So you think I'm an ass. Can you tell me why?

OLA   Of course I can. You sit in a cage doing nothing. Daddy said at lunch you're a scrounger.

HUNGER ARTIST   Come closer. I'll tell you who I am. It's a fact that I have nothing to offer people apart from my hunger. Your daddy is right, I am a scrounger, but a scrounger who fasts, who doesn't eat your portions. Which of you stuck out her tongue at me?

MONICA   She did.

HUNGER ARTIST   You were right to stick your tongue out at me.

THE BAND is beginning to practise a march for tomorrow's ceremony.

GUARD I   (*shouting and moving towards the cage*) Hey, girls, move away from the cage. You didn't by any chance throw any food into the cage? Feeding the Hunger Artist is strictly forbidden!

MONICA   He can't eat flowers and stems.

GUARD I   Push off! Straightaway! Get a move on! (*turning to THE HUNGER ARTIST*) And as for you, don't try anything with the children, it's not proper.

IMPRESARIO (*comes over to the cage, places a folding chair next to* THE HUNGER ARTIST *who moistens his lips with water*) Get ready, friend, the fun ends tomorrow. But please don't play any tricks, don't fuss, don't resist. I know you can fast for another forty days. I know and you know but for the people forty days of waiting, that's the limit of their endurance. Once again I've got to tell you it's too much, too long. People now are impatient. '*Es waren andere Zeiten*'. Dearest Ernest. I'm wondering whether to shorten the fast to 33 or even 30 days. Don't get upset. It's not my fault times are changing. You look at me with such fury and contempt, as if I were trying to snatch some treasure from you. Can't you understand my position, my friend. (*throughout this long monologue the orchestra practises a march, so only fragments of THE IMPRESARIO's speech can be heard*) If it's forty days, no one bothers to follow and check whether a chap is really fasting or cheating. You would have to put someone like Hitler inside and in any case, in Europe alone there are now a dozen or so hunger artists who fast more effectively and faster than you do. They also have better social graces. They know foreign languages, they appear at festivals and banquets, they don't have your arrogance, they love everyone, they understand everybody. After the fasts they go to first class restaurants and even embassies. I know what you want to say. It's true, during their fasts they take small quantities of concentrated foods like those that cosmonauts eat. That's a fact. People know about it but don't take it seriously. They pretend everything is quite in order. They even prefer false hunger artists, because they are more human, more like them, they can be understood!

It's the last time, Ernest. People haven't got the time to spend forty days thinking about your fasting. They grow suspicious and hostile, they think you despise them. Please don't let me down tomorrow. Behave like a normal human being. Smile, say a few words, tell a funny story or make a friendly gesture. You are a loner, alienated. You think nothing is more important than your fasting. You'll end up being a figure of fun. Yes, funny, boring, pretentious. Look around you, in 1974 the world's population has grown to three billion 890 million, which means a growth of 72 million people in a single year! If this rate of growth is kept up, the number of people on earth will double in 36 years.

I'm trying to understand you and the sense behind your fasting. I am well disposed. After all, one could say that you are

103

supporting me and my wife — but it isn't as simple as that. We provide the framework for your persona, your fasting. Without that framework, those prosaic accessories which you despise you wouldn't even begin to exist. People don't just fast — they even die of hunger — but they die without publicity and of course not of their own will. They are the only true hunger artists. But you, Ernest, you are a professional Hunger Artist. You have orders of merit and university honours. In fact, you are one of the false fasting showmen and your isolation is arrogance in disguise. Some years before I met you I was manager to a monkey — don't laugh — that's not quite accurate, in fact it was a chimp who, thanks to his strong will, achieved such perfection that he not only appeared in Variety but acquired human speech. Finally, at the apex of his career and development, when it was possible to regard him as something approaching a human being, he gave a famous lecture to members of the Academy. My friend, I shall never forget his first words. I shall never forget when he stood at the lectern with a microphone, a glass and a sparkling jug of water and he said in his low, warm, somewhat rasping voice: 'Hohe Herren von der Akademie! ...'

THE IMPRESARIO bows his head, lost in thought. Gets up and goes towards the box-office where one or two people are buying tickets. THE IMPRESARIO enters the kiosk. His head now appears next to his WIFE's. THE IMPRESARIO is chewing a toothpick and talks through it.

IMPRESARIO What are the takings today?

WIFE Three crowns.

IMPRESARIO In a word, one schoolboy, two invalids and a soldier. Won't be enough for the Hunger Artist's straw.

WIFE Take out that toothpick.

IMPRESARIO This is all I've been eating these last few days. We must ask our benefactor to swap roles with me. Let him take over my job and I'll crawl into the cage. You will be able to parade me, a freak, a man, a real ox feeding on toothpicks! Ha ha ha ha ha ha!

WIFE What's this bellowing?

IMPRESARIO I'm wondering whether we shouldn't provoke a punchup. Because if they don't show any interest tomorrow, we won't even see a lame dog. See those on the bench, drinking beer and intending to go on drinking? I'll give them a crown and they'll create such a rave-up half the town will be here.

WIFE   I don't know ...

IMPRESARIO   I say, boys, do you want to earn something?

GUARD 1   Learn? Learning is for fools.

IMPRESARIO   Not learn – *earn.*

GUARD 1   Oh well, in that case. That's alright, governor.

IMPRESARIO   Come over here, I'll tell you what I have in mind ...

GUARD 2   Please join us.

THE IMPRESARIO goes to the bench and sits next to the 'layabouts': people who know their rights but prefer not to know their duties. THE IMPRESARIO bends over and explains something in a whisper. The layabouts nod their heads. THE IMPRESARIO gives them a coin and walks over to the box-office. A FATHER and SON come up to the cage.

SON   Why are we standing here?

FATHER   Do you see that gentleman sitting on the straw?

SON   Yes.

FATHER   And do you see what's written on the board?

SON   Yes, the figure 39.

FATHER   It means this gentleman hasn't been eating for 39 days. Remember that.

SON   And no one gets angry with him?

FATHER   No, because this gentleman fasts in order to be famous. He gets paid. He is an extraordinary man.

SON   They give him money because he doesn't want to eat? And all the time you shout at me 'eat, eat, eat'.

FATHER   Shut up!

THE MOTHER enters from the other side of the cage, she talks very precisely and distinctly – she does not mince her words.

MOTHER   Listen, I'm not sure that it's wise to show children a man who refuses to eat.

FATHER   He's stirred.

MOTHER   And so what? It's quite natural for a living man to move. Must you always find unsuitable amusements? A child ought to be brought up in such a manner as to make his way in the real world. If somebody likes fasting, that's his own private business. In times when whole tribes die of hunger, when I have to queue endlessly to buy a few ounces of ham or steak, it's indelicate of men to show their fasting.

SON   Does the Hunger Artist go to the lavatory like we do?

MOTHER   (*hitting the boy on the hands*) Don't ask stupid questions! (*turning to her husband*) We are gathering the first fruits of your educational methods.

FATHER   Don't you know he fasts voluntarily? With the money he makes he can eat out in places like the Ritz or the Savoy.

MOTHER   And he probably eats ... you know ... I heard funny stories about him ... they say he's been put up for propaganda purposes by ... well you know who. I can't talk in front of the child.

While this conversation is going on, the characters bribed by THE IMPRESARIO stage a simulated punch-up outside the box-office. The HUNGER ARTIST who has been dozing, wakes up. He hears voices and cries.

VOICES   I've been queueing in front of you, I only went away for a minute ... this lady will vouch for me ... this lady stood in front of me ... I've been standing here all morning before they opened the box-office ... keep this woman out of the argument ... if you were queueing you shouldn't have gone away ... my grey hair ... babe in arms ... the bloody brute ... I've never seen this woman ... Haven't they had enough of the war and the occupation ... For Chrissake, what is it we are queueing for ... some show ... corn-ointment for dogs ... a pack of lies ... slimming foods ... I don't believe in these ointments ... I've been rubbing my head for a whole year, I keep explaining to you like a child, this was my place, and you keep on ... three tickets for the front row ... hands off ... they are showing the Hunger Artist ... what does he do? ... doesn't do anything ... if he doesn't do anything, what do they show? God, what a primitive bunch! thirty years after the war ... call the police ... call a doctor ... we need a priest ... eh, look over there, there in the trees! A cross ... a cross in the spruce tree ... let's pray ... you blind? Can't you see the cross right at the top? ... crazy bitch ...

THE HUNGER ARTIST *rises, lifts up his arms, opens his mouth wide but no sound comes.* THE CROWD *consists of all the actors who have already appeared:* THE OLD BOY *in the track-suit, two girls in shorts and vests,* GUARDS, LAYABOUTS, CHILDREN, *etc.*

9: THE HUNGER ARTIST DEPARTS

The cage is hidden in a tightly fitting grey covering like a hood. THE GUARDS unroll a red carpet which leads from the cage through the whole stage to the park path. Brass band playing in the bowl. The stage is surrounded by a small audience. They are the same actors who have already appeared previously. THE IMPRESARIO bows.

IMPRESARIO (*bowing*) My Lord Mayor, ladies and gentlemen, dear children, friends. In a moment the solemn hour will strike. Our great Hunger Artist, the unique and last authentic Hunger Artist, is about to conclude his forty-day fast and in a moment will sit down to a repast. A repast devised by outstanding medical practitioners which will enable the Hunger Artist's body to return to us, to our humdrum and yet wonderful life. It may be that in these times of crematoria, annihilation camps, terror, bomb outrages, and cosmic flights, voluntary fasting is no longer as attractive as it had been in the days of our parents and grandparents. Whole races die of hunger and whole continents starve and are undernourished. Therefore all the more worthy of our admiration is a man who, in an insignificant and unattractive manner, wishes to illumine our humdrum grey existence with his wonderful gift. In a moment the seals will be broken on the locks and in a triumphal procession we shall lead a man who has risen above his times and whose acts, though perhaps not as spectacular as those of the astronauts, give us yet an inkling of what man's potential is. My Lord Mayor, I request you to cut the ribbon and open the festivities. Girls!

THE IMPRESARIO claps his hands. OLA and MONICA unfurl the ribbon in front of THE MAYOR. THE MAYOR cuts the ribbon with nail scissors which he has pulled out of his pocket. Here and there an occasional shout. THE LORD MAYOR, THE IMPRESARIO, THE GUARDS and THE GIRLS approach the cage. Suddenly in the silence the muffled singing of THE HUNGER ARTIST.

HUNGER ARTIST   (*sings*) Poor Rover from the kitchen slab
   Did steal some juicy meat
   A cruel stupid cook went mad
   And killed him for this feat

THE IMPRESARIO rushes to the cage and with a single movement pulls off the hood. The cage is revealed covered in garlands of green shoots and multi-coloured flowers. THE HUNGER ARTIST is standing in the cage and sings:

HUNGER ARTIST   (*sings*) Another much more kindly cook
   Who Rover's slaughter saw
   Set up a splendid tombstone there
   Which this inscription bore:

Laughter breaks out all round. Someone throws a rotten tomato, someone else an egg. The band is playing a march. THE GUARDS and THE GIRLS approach the cage door. THE GUARDS open the door, THE HUNGER ARTIST stands at the door. He remains motionless, then retreats into the cage. THE IMPRESARIO follows THE HUNGER ARTIST and forcibly, but with well-mannered gestures, pushes him out of the cage and on to the path. He stands behind THE HUNGER ARTIST. Now THE GIRLS approach THE HUNGER ARTIST, take him by the hands and lead him towards the table. THE HUNGER ARTIST resists but THE IMPRESARIO pushes him from behind with his knee. THE HUNGER ARTIST is dressed in an unfashionable best suit — dark with white stripes — too broad at the shoulders, with sleeves above the wrists. But he has a fashionable bright tie with a huge knot. His lips are painted dark blue, his hair greasy, shiny and stuck down. THE GIRLS sit THE HUNGER ARTIST down at a tiny table, curtsy beautifully in front of him and gesture him to eat.

HUNGER ARTIST   (*lifting his arms*) Allow me to depart today at this
   hour in front of these people who eat. I confess that my fasting is
   the height of conceit and arrogance. I ask you all to forgive me
   … allow me to depart … I will not disturb your quiet well-
   earned digestion of food, music and song … thank you for your
   patience and courtesy which I have not deserved.

THE END

PS   FROM MY WORKSHOP

I am moving further and further away from The *Hungerkünstler* but I still feel ties which constrain me. Only a few threads bind me to the story. My Hunger Artist is very distant from that dumb Hunger Artist in a black leotard. My Hunger Artist talks a lot, both in 'verse' and in 'prose'. In Kafka only in the last section of the story do we hear a conversation. It's a short dialogue between the Hunger Artist and his overseer who had dug the Hunger Artist up from rotting straw. No one had remembered his existence any more.

– Are you still fasting? When on earth do you mean to stop?
    – Forgive me, everybody.
    – Of course we forgive you.
    – I always wanted you to admire my fasting.
    – We do admire it.
    – But you shouldn't admire it.
    – Well then, we don't admire it ... but why shouldn't we admire it?
    – Because I have to fast, I can't do anything else.
    – What a fellow you are ... and why can't you do anything else?
    – Because ... because I couldn't find any food I liked. If I had found any, believe me, I should have made no bones about it and stuffed myself like you or anyone else.

These were the Hunger Artist's last words. The difficulty lay and still lies in the fact that I had to place in the mouths of characters appearing in the story (and also those I called to life) words which Kafka had not written and this had been my stumbling block for many years. There are carefree writers who put their words, thoughts and styles into the mouths of Jesus, Caesar, Napoleon, and Mickiewicz whom they claim to have created. We have many such brave fellows. As far as I am concerned, however, Jesus speaking in the language of a litterateur from Warsaw, Poznań or Zakopane is a transgression. Only pride (not humility) can bring about such 'works' but these lordly fellows find applause and recognition even among the faithful. So I forgive and ask forgiveness. Franz Kafka himself, who was one of the great authentic Hunger Artists, would never condemn 'normal' people who marry, furnish flats and have children (let us not forget the sympathy that Kafka had for fatties). He admired their liveliness and he despised his own body, his emaciated covering.

At night I slept very badly. Lying awake I yearned for daylight. I trusted it would bring a solution. I was reading *Ein Bericht für eine Akademie*. While writing 'The Hunger Artist Departs' I was recalling Kafka's (theatrical?) 'rehearsals' ('attempts'). In his one and only 'play' the action slowly dies away and eventually comes to a halt. The pulse of a dying drama?

Which way leads to the Hunger Artist? Through which gate am I to enter the interior? where is my entrance? I have to create it myself. Perhaps everything is open and therefore there is no need to seek a special entrance (exit)? Someone bold and innocent will enter there with a light step and rearrange everything. It is of course Kafka's excellence which had blocked all entrances.